# Dog and Pony Show

## Two Veterinarians, One Story

John H. Hunt, DVM
David A. Jefferson, DVM

# Dog and Pony Show
## Two Veterinarians, One Story

**Copyright ©2021 by Dr John H. Hunt and Dr David A. Jefferson**

All rights reserved. No part of this work may be reproduced or transmitted in any form or by any means, electrical or mechanical, including photocopying and recording, or by any information storage or retrieval system, except with written permission from the authors.

You may contact John Hunt at *JohnHunt52@icloud.com*
or his blog: *dogcatadvice.com*
and David Jefferson at: *dajdvm@maine.rr.com*
or his blog: *www.horsehealthwithdrj.com*

Edited for Dr Hunt: Jane Hunt Tucker

Edited for Dr Jefferson: Carla McAllister

Cover design by Elizabeth Soucie

Photographs used in this book were provided by the authors.

ISBN 979-8785843899

Printed in the United States of America

*PRGott Books Publishing Service*
Norway, Maine
www.prgottbooks.net

# Dedication

To Peg Wheeler, MS, LVT,
pioneer, educator, listener, advisor, and friend
to her students and her faculty

# Other Books by:

## Dr Hunt

*Ask the Vet*

*Enjoy Your Pet and Don't Forget to Give them a Hug*

*Why does My Cat Look At Me Like That?*
    Ponderings of A Small Town Veterinarian

Short Story:
    *Strange Happenings in Bailey's Mistake*

~ books available at *dogcatadvice.com*

## Dr Jefferson

*Maine Horse Doctor*
    On the Road with Dr J

*Goodbye Old Friend*
    The Euthanasia of Your Horse

~ books available at *www.HorsehealthwithDrJ.com*

# Table of Contents

Copyright ............................................................ 2
Dedication .......................................................... 3
Other Books by Dr Hunt and Dr Jefferson ....... 4
Table of Contents ............................................. 5
Acknowledgements ........................................... 7
Foreword ............................................................ 9
Chapter 1   Discovering Veterinary Medicine ................ 11
   Dr Hunt: My Path to Vet School ............................... 13
   Dr Jefferson: Beginnings ............................................ 19
Chapter 2   Veterinary School ........................................ 25
   Dr Hunt: Vet School Highlight Reel (Bloopers) ....... 27
   Dr Jefferson: Four Years at Cornell Vet School ........ 36
Chapter 3   Getting a Job ................................................ 43
   Dr Hunt: The Interviews ............................................ 45
   Dr Jefferson: The Job Offer ....................................... 50
Chapter 4   The Early Years ............................................ 53
   Dr Hunt: Pretending to be a Vet ............................... 55
   Dr Jefferson: My First Job ......................................... 60
Chapter 5   Influencers .................................................... 67
   Dr Hunt: My Pinball Life ........................................... 69
   Dr Jefferson: My Mentors ......................................... 73
Chapter 6   A Dangerous Profession ............................. 77
   Dr Hunt: Staying Safe ................................................ 79
   Dr Jefferson: It Goes with the Job ............................ 86
Chapter 7   Prevention .................................................... 89
   Dr Hunt: Kooties ........................................................ 91
   Dr Jefferson: Farm Animals and Epidemics ............ 95
Chapter 8   Vets Cry, Too ................................................ 99
   Dr Hunt: Vets are Pet Owners, Too ......................... 101
   Dr Jefferson: My Deep Loss ...................................... 103

# Table of Contents, cont.

| | |
|---|---|
| Chapter 9  OOPS | 107 |
|   Dr Hunt: A Slip of the Scalpel and Other Mishaps | 109 |
|   Dr Jefferson: My Mistake | 113 |
| Chapter 10  Final Goodbye | 117 |
|   Dr Hunt: Peaceful Death | 119 |
|   Dr Jefferson: Old Red | 122 |
| Chapter 11  Wake Up Call | 125 |
|   Dr Hunt: My Big Injury that Threatened My Practice | 127 |
|   Dr Jefferson: Big Doors Swing on Small Hinges | 131 |
| Chapter 12  Funny Stories | 135 |
|   Dr Hunt: Finding Humor in My Job | 137 |
|   Dr Jefferson: The Wedding Ring | 142 |
| Chapter 13  Memorable Clients | 149 |
|   Dr Hunt: Clients, the Other Half of Vet Medicine | 151 |
|   Dr Jefferson: Best Friend Forever | 155 |
| Chapter 14  Kids | 159 |
|   Dr Hunt: Career Day | 161 |
|   Dr Jefferson: Life Lesson | 163 |
| Chapter 15  EMERGENCY! | 167 |
|   Dr Hunt: The Dreaded Late Night Phone Call | 169 |
|   Dr Jefferson: Call from Hell | 172 |
| Chapter 16  Home Remedies | 179 |
|   Dr Hunt: Long Held Beliefs | 181 |
|   Dr Jefferson: Equine Traditions | 185 |
| Chapter 17  Out to Pasture | 189 |
|   Dr Hunt: Next Phase | 191 |
|   Dr Jefferson: A New Career or Two | 193 |
| About the Author(s) | 195 |
|   Dr Hunt | 197 |
|   Dr Jefferson | 199 |

# Acknowledgements

To Pat Gott for her willingness to take on this team project and to her business partner, Laura Ashton, for her suggestions and setting up the final work for publishing. To Elizabeth Soucie for the cover and back designs and her technical expertise throughout. To our clients whose love of animals has meant meaningful careers for both of us.

from Dr Hunt:

Thank you to Dave, my coauthor, for his friendship, guidance, input, constructive criticism and being my number one fan. We never shared a cross word. It has been a fun experience that I would do again with him in a heartbeat. Thanks to my wife, Michelle, for her support and patience. I also thank my daughter, Jane, for editing my stories, even while raising a newborn.

from Dr Jefferson:

To John who birthed this idea and was so much fun to work with. To my wife, Bonnie, for her willingness to listen, advise, and insert all the missing commas.

# Foreword

Dave and I first met as teachers in the veterinary technician program at York County Community College in Wells, Maine. We hit it off almost immediately during a help session for instructors on Brightspace, a new learning platform. We didn't have a clue what was going on nor were we really interested in learning, so we got to know each other during class. We were very bad students.

We used to meet in the college cafeteria during the school year to discuss our student's progress, teaching issues and the books we were writing. One day our fearless leader, Peg Wheeler, the director of the Animal Health Technician program told us that she was looking for an instructor for the spring semester class, Animal Diseases. David and I looked at each other knowing this was a trap. Peg was trying to recruit one of us. That is what directors do, lure unsuspecting would-be teachers into teaching and Peg was a master. She said the instructor can teach anything he wants in any way he wants. That was the baited hook she threw out because teaching takes a lot of time, commitment with hardly any pay. I could see David was thinking about it, but he turned on a dime and calmly explained he goes to Florida from January to March and besides, he doesn't know anything about small animal diseases. I detected a slight sigh of relief. Peg turned to me. I blurted out, stealing Dave's excuse, "I don't know anything about large animal diseases."

Peg is not one to give up so easily. She said in her calm alluring tone, like the Sirens of Ulysses, "You can teach any disease you want." Damn, she had me.

Now I am not known to think quickly on my feet, but I surprised myself and responded, "But I go to Florida in March."

Peg lowered her eyes and walked away as if she were defeated. We love Peg, she built the program from scratch and will do anything for the students. As Dave and I watched Peg walk away seemingly defeated we knew we had to help her out.

Dave said, "Hey John, why don't you teach the first half of the course covering small animal diseases, then when I return from Florida I'll take over and teach large animal diseases so you can go to Florida." When we walked over to Peg to tell her the news, she gave us smile of relief and gratitude but her eyes told me this was all calculated. Like I said, she is good at what she does.

For three years Dave and I used our personal experiences as veterinarians to teach students about diseases. The students were treated with personal, real stories about medical cases from a small animal and large animal perspective. As we collaborated it came to us that maybe writing a book about our journey through vet medicine comparing large animal and small animal medicine would be fun. Dave claims this was my idea. I'm not going to be the fall guy here. If this book tanks, we both go down with the ship together!

Our goal was to tell our personal stories side by side so our readers get a true feel of how different practicing veterinary medicine can be yet how similar they were. Losing a patient, early years, mistakes, client relationships are all very similar regardless of what kind of animal you treat. Yet treating a horse medically is so much different than a dog.

The process of writing a book with someone else was new to Dave and me. If we didn't like each other this book would not have been written. The other remarkable ingredient was that we love each other's writing. We are each other's biggest fan! Right up through actual publishing we have been able to agree on how it should look and what the content should be. We have been in touch mostly by email with chapters going back and forth. There is the occasional phone call to check on progress. Dave set up a long table in his den so he could lay out the book. When I saw a picture of the table it looked like "52-card pickup", piles of paper strewn everywhere. He assured me it was logical and well organized. I had to take his word for it.

I suggested we share our thoughts about the other's writing at the end of each chapter. Critiquing our partner's chapters was fun because we love the other's style and welcomed the chance to rib each other. We call it "Afterthoughts." It gave us the chance to make comments, share more stories, and tease each other. We also both like to have the last word. Afterthoughts is a window into our friendship both professional and personal. Enjoy them!

We hope you will enjoy learning how we navigated our profession as much as we did writing about it.

John H. Hunt, DVM

# Chapter 1

## Discovering Veterinary Medicine

# Dr Hunt: My Path to Vet School

"John, you're not smart enough."

That was what I was told by one of the professors on my master's degree committee just before I defended my thesis paper. He must have gotten the short straw. I can't imagine any of my committee members wanting to tell me I wasn't invited to continue on in the zoology doctoral program at Michigan State University.

I felt a sense of foreboding as I entered his office, his desk piled high with manuscripts and his bookcases along the walls strewn haphazardly with books. The dirty windows behind the desk created a muted light like thunderclouds moving overhead. Dr Bing had to wheel his chair from around his desk to see me as I nervously sat down on a metal chair used in classrooms. Even seated he loomed over me, a tall, thin man with a long face and pointed nose—like a scarecrow without a straw hat. His face revealed a worried, sad, nervous look as he leaned forward to tell me something that I was not prepared or expecting to hear: "You can't continue here because you aren't smart enough." I was slack jawed. What the hell was he talking about? I had no response. For a few seconds I simply stared at him in disbelief. It felt like I got struck by lightning. How could I defend myself? I couldn't. I didn't. I got up, thanked him (for what, I don't know), and walked out, not knowing at the time that this was the beginning of my journey on becoming a veterinarian.

As a youngster, I grew up in the rural suburbs of Chicago. I didn't have a lifelong goal of being a veterinarian. As a matter of fact, I never even knew our family veterinarian in Chicago. I do not recall my father ever going to the vet. Maybe that is why we always had a herd of outdoor cats hanging around that my dad was forever trying to give away. When I was ten, we moved to Dobbs Ferry, New York. I went with my dad several times to see our vet, Dr Steddy. My mom was disenchanted with Dr Steddy; she did not like him because one of our dogs hated him. To be honest, the time I went with my dad for a routine call for Lady, our Lab, she was a complete boob. What I saw was the vet having to manhandle Lady up onto the exam table and continue to sit on her to keep her on the table. Experiences like those did not leave me with a warm and fuzzy feeling about being a vet. When Mom heard "how Lady was treated," she immediately assumed Lady did not like the vet. As a veterinarian, I now appreciate what Dr Steddy was dealing with—a dog that was simply scared stiff—literally. Lady kept her legs straight and stiff, thrashed her head around, and arched her thorax back and forth like an earthworm. Poor Dr Steddy could barely get a physical done. I've had clients in my practice declare their dog or cat didn't like Dr Hunt. I must admit there were times that might have been true. I may also have been a scapegoat for justifying a pet's bad behavior. Sorry Mom, but I just threw you under the bus.

It's not like I didn't have animals while growing up. We had all sorts of pets: dogs, cats, tropical fish, guinea pigs, turtles, ducks, chameleons, frogs, and even lightning bugs. Heck, my older sister had cockroaches for a little while. They were test subjects for a science project she had in high school. Dad took the brunt of pet care, since when the Hunt kids were given the task of taking care of a pet, it did not turn out so well. For example, we all got a painted turtle to care for. We each had a pie pan-shaped plastic container with a molded ramp ending at a small platform in the middle. A plastic palm tree stuck up on the platform like a flagpole. Our job was to keep the water clean and to feed the turtles. Well, we overfed them with turtle food and lettuce, which made for a primordial soup in the water (water that we did not change half as much as we should have). We would play with the turtles on the living room rug. Later that day my mom would find them under the couch when she was doing the house cleaning. Poor turtles. Poor Mom! By default, I did start to take care of our pets when I was in junior high school. My older sibs were in high school and had other more important things to do. My dad was only too happy to relinquish those responsibilities.

There was a small swamp down the street in Chicago where I used to go with my two older brothers—this is where we caught frogs. We spent hours there catching polliwogs, looking for animals, trying to spear fish, or spearing each other with cattail stems. My brothers would throw cherry bombs in the water or throw large rocks to make splashes reminiscent of the torpedoes that exploded in our favorite WWII movies. Crawling on our bellies in the swamp grass and making forts were favorite games. We often returned home wet and muddy and usually right before my mom was trying to prepare for a dinner party hosting my dad's faculty colleagues from the University of Chicago. You would think growing up in a house rich with animals, being one with nature in a swamp, and caring for our dogs would lead me to veterinary medicine, but that was not the case.

The fond memories of muck and cattails and the environmental movement in the late 1960s won me over. I selected the University of Connecticut with the goal of studying ecology and natural resources. Courses like ornithology, mammalogy, botany, forest ecology, dendrology, and soil science armed me with the knowledge to go out and save our environment. As a senior, however, I realized there were no jobs in world saving. I loved college, so I decided to go to graduate school in zoology, specifically animal behavior. That way I could teach and save the world through research.

After being shown the door at grad school, my friend and I decided the Peace Corp would be a good idea. I guess I had a compunction to set the world straight in another country. We applied together. He got assigned to study monkeys in the El Salvador jungles, and I was initially assigned to Kuala Lumpur to do God knows what. I went home to NY to await further instructions, but I never heard from them. My life would have been so much different if I had.

I spent the next year living with my folks back in Dobbs Ferry. During that year I worked part time at a college library and was the first girls' track and field coach for my old high school. I substitute taught at the high school and I taught a biology class at a local small college, Mercy College. It was an evening class filled with older, working students. I think at 24, I was the youngest person in class. I wore an old corduroy jacket and a tie to make myself look older or more official. After a few lectures, the class figured I knew what I was talking about, and they began to take me seriously.

That was not my first teaching gig. I was a teaching assistant at MSU while in graduate school, where I taught introductory biology labs. I also had to sit in on televised lectures shown in campus dorms and answer questions the students had about the material. That was nerve racking and distracting because I had to explain someone else's lecture to sleepy, pajama-clad freshmen who overslept and came in late with their coffee and cinnamon buns.

I loved teaching at MSU. The bio labs were fun and challenging. I could teach them any way I wanted just as long as I covered the topics for the course. Grading and prep work took a lot of time. Back then we still used the old mimeograph to print copies of our tests and assignments. There was only one in the office, so being on the good side of the secretaries was a must. I knew when the mimeograph was being used well before entering the office—the smell of the ink permeated the hallways. It was like sniffing airplane glue. I knew it was bad to inhale the solvent vapors, but you couldn't help it. And besides, it smelled good. There were about ten TAs for this course of about 2000 students. On Fridays, the TAs had a meeting with the TA coordinator at a local pub in East Lansing. He realized that he had better get all of what he had to say before the second round of beer pitchers were ordered. You can see why I liked teaching bio labs at MSU! The reason I had wanted to get a PhD was because I liked research and teaching, and high school teaching positions were non-existent in the mid-70s. I had a good role model, too—my dad was a professor of psychology.

So, there I was, at home, living with my parents and doing what I loved to do, teaching and coaching, but they were part time, dead-end jobs, so I applied to the NY State Cooperative Extension Agency. As a cooperative extension agent, I would help the public through instruction and continuing education in agriculture, natural resources, or whatever else I was qualified to do. For weeks I heard nothing. I was getting discouraged. I felt lost and directionless. It was time to get help from Dad, the go-to guy. He was a professor of psychology at Columbia University, knew three languages, and was generally brilliant. As kids we would play the dictionary game, where we selected any word in the dictionary and he would give the meaning. Little did I know at the time that he could figure out the definition by knowing the Latin or Greek roots of the word. Up to this point he had stayed out of my career development. I think his minimum requirement was that I wasn't lying around the house watching TV.

*Dog and Pony Show*

    I went down to our large Victorian-style kitchen with its high ceilings and walk-in fireplace where we had a long, drop leaf dinner table. Dad had his chair at the end where he spent his mornings sipping coffee, reading the New York Times and fiddling with his pipe. His pipe was like an extension of his thought process. When I talked with him he would play with the pipe while he was talking or thinking. He used to rub the pipe on his nose—to keep the wood well oiled. He would also tap the tobacco in the bowl, scrape out the bowl with a special scraper, or run a pipe cleaner through the stem. It was comforting to see him perform all these little tasks because that meant his mind was engaged. My dad was soft spoken, except when the three Hunt boys were being "disobedient" as he used to proclaim. During our conversation, he was non-judgmental and did not try to tell me the kind of job I should get. Rather, he asked me questions about myself and what I liked to do. Then we put our heads together to try and think of a profession that fit. I wanted to teach, I wanted to do something with animals or ecology, and I wanted a challenging job that could support me. My dad brought up veterinary medicine. That never even occurred to me. A veterinarian teaches, researches, and works with animals and people—all the interests I had been pursuing in a piecemeal fashion in one job. With a veterinary degree, my options were limitless. So, sitting at our kitchen table on a Sunday afternoon, I decided to become a veterinarian.

    I had no idea how hard it was to get in. Back then there were only 17 vet schools in the entire country. On top of that, if your state did not have a vet school, only a few seats were reserved at vet schools nearby. For instance, Maine, which had no vet school, had two seats for Cornell. Two! For the entire state! To make things more complicated for me, since I lived in a state that did have a vet school, I could only apply to that vet school. I really wanted to go back to Michigan and try to get into MSU rather than go to the NY vet school at Cornell. I felt I had roots in Michigan. I lived in Michigan for over three years during graduate school, my parents were from Michigan, and my grandfather was a professor at MSU. Even though my tenure as a grad student ended on a sour note, my time there was fabulous. I loved the campus, made a lot of friends, and in spite of academia politics, I got a good education. I decided to pack up my clothes and head for Michigan to reestablish my residency. The day after I decided to head for Michigan, the NY State Cooperative Extension Agency called me to come in for an interview. My mind was made up, though—Michigan or bust. Soon thereafter I was told I had to have straight A's to get into vet school, and even then, I would have been competing with over 500 applicants for 100 openings. I was far from an A student. YIKES! What was I thinking?

Before making the momentous step to move back to Michigan, I thought it prudent to at least visit a veterinary office in NY to see if I had problems with allergies or if I would pass out on the floor watching a routine surgery. A small animal vet in nearby Yonkers was kind enough to let me observe. I enjoyed the atmosphere and all the things that went on behind the scenes, like running lab tests, treating hospitalized patients, and taking x-rays. The first time I watched a surgery I was fascinated rather than nauseous. It was a go. The 14-hour drive to Michigan in my Corvair with a bench seat, plastic seat cover and a radio that just got Christian channels was the easy part.

I spent almost a year in Michigan working for several veterinary clinics and taking courses required by the vet school like poultry science and cow production. The odds of getting into vet school were astronomical, but I applied and was accepted into the class of 1982. I had a fantasy of walking into my graduate school professor's office and telling him, "Not bad for someone who was told 'John, you're not smart enough'."

\* \* \* \*

Afterthoughts by Dr Jefferson:

"Not smart enough." Wow, that statement by someone on a committee that determines your future would have knocked my socks off! Then the Peace Corps never gets back to him! It's a testament to John's character that he didn't pack it in and decide against any more college. I like the scene of his dad stroking a pipe and pondering John's future. Great wisdom. He considered John's strengths, then came up with the idea of veterinary medicine. Perfect fit!

## Dr Jefferson: Beginnings

Two things are true for me. I have always been fascinated with animals and, no matter what the weather, I would rather be out there than in here.

Given those preferences, I guess it was logical for me to think about becoming a farmer. The idea of becoming a vet didn't come until later, much later. Who has more contact with animals than dairy farmers? As a milk producer each cow gets personally handled twice a day. I'm not sure where the idea about me farming came from, because I had never really talked to a farmer. There was no access. I grew up in the suburbs of New York City. Our one and only animal was a cat named Toby. My father was one of many who took the commuter train into the city every day. In our bedroom community of Pelham, New York, it was assumed by parents and teachers that after you graduated, your next step was college. Then, the expectation was that you would ride the train every day into the city, and do something in one of those tall buildings so you could afford to live here as an adult. I talked to an advisor in high school about farming. His response was "A farmer? ... as, like ... on a farm? ... Why? "

I was 14, and it was time to see if this was a just a pipe dream. A friend of a friend told my family about someone they knew who owned a dairy farm. Letters were written, phone calls made, and it was arranged that I would job shadow that summer. Mom dropped me off at the farm in Putney, Vermont, and said she'd pick me up in late August. I'm sure she hoped the summer would kill my dream. Over the next three months I learned how to milk cows and how to operate a tractor. I learned how to stack hay on a wagon so it wouldn't come off on the way to the barn. It's no fun doing that job twice. Everything was new and exciting for this kid from the suburbs. I remember watching, open-mouthed, as their large animal vet performed a rectal exam on a cow, his arm up to his shoulder, deep, deep inside her. I had no idea what he was doing and was quite shy, so I didn't ask any questions, but, I was intrigued. Why was he doing that? What was he feeling in there? That I would someday be doing the same thing never entered my head.

My time off was Sundays in between the two milkings. There was no one my age on the farm or in the area, but they had a farm dog named Scooter that went everywhere with me and became my pal. On hot days we would walk to a small pond for a swim. I learned not to go underwater. The spring-fed water was so cold it gave me a headache. After a swim we sat on the grassy bank, kicked back and just enjoyed the sun. I learned how to drive and shift gears in the old Apache Chevy pickup with four on the floor. I had my first taste of something alcoholic— I was offered some "apple jack." I thought it was just cider, but after half a glass the room began to tip. The whole summer was a wonderful exposure to everything I love about New England farm life.

The farm had a bull. Dairy bulls are incredibly strong and very unpredictable. This one's name was George. He weighed over a ton with a huge neck and chest. His attitude was, "Come on into my space, I dare you!" There was a 55-gallon steel drum in his paddock that he liked to get his head under and toss into the air. His enclosure filled the space between two large barns. It was much quicker to cut through George's paddock than to walk all the way around to get from one barn to the other. I was young, pretty fast, and when no one was around to say no, I used his paddock as a short cut. I would climb the fence on one side and head for the fence on the other. It was about 30 yards between the two fences. The speed of my crossing depended on exactly where George was in the paddock. I'd walk if he was at the far end of the paddock and run if he was closer. I always kept one eye on him. One day I thought he was in the shadow of the overhang of his barn. My mistake. It turned out that he was about 20 yards from me, in the other direction, not visible because I was looking into the sun. I was walking, keeping my eye out for him in the dark overhang when I felt the ground shake behind me. I looked over my shoulder and saw him coming on a dead run toward me, head down, ready to toss me like that steel drum. I have never run as fast, before or since, as I did in those 5 seconds. I scrambled up the five-foot fence on the other side like a monkey. Just as my second leg went over the top, his forehead hit the fence. There was a crack like a gunshot, and the rough cut 2x12 inch plank broke in two. The impact rocked the fence and sent me flying to the ground six feet away. It was no surprise to me to learn years later in agriculture college that the North American dairy bull is responsible for more human deaths than all other animal encounters combined, including wild carnivores and rabid dogs.

I was 17 when I spent a summer on another dairy farm in Duchess County, New York. I was stronger and a bit more useful. That farm was up to date with a milking parlor. I milked cows every morning starting at five and again every evening until around six. In between milkings there was hay to mow, rake, and bale, and machinery to grease. I had been accepted in the two-year dairy program at Delhi Tech, New York, that coming September and was anxious to learn all I could before my freshman year started. I was sure my future was with cattle, so I spent a lot of time with the cows. I was learning about animal individuality. Annie was always the first cow to enter the parlor in the morning, and again for the late afternoon milking. She made it clear that this was her right. Suzanna, on the other hand, was always last and wouldn't make a move to enter unless I walked behind her to urge her in. There was Betty, who loved to have her butt scratched and Penny who resented being touched. "Sure, go ahead and take my milk, but leave me be!"

I genuinely liked the classes at Delhi. It was all usable information and, for the first time, studying became something I wanted to do. I was hungry, and the studying, unlike high school, became more than a way to pass an exam. I just wanted to learn. After graduation I was hired to manage a small milking herd for a local businessman. It was a taste of what having my own farm would be like. Within a few months, I became restless. It wasn't my farm, and they weren't my cows. I began to wonder how I could ever afford a place of my own. I also found milking cows twice a day, with no days off, restricting. Was this really to be my future? One morning after the cows were milked and the chores were done, I drove the half hour from Delhi to Oneonta, New York, where recruiters from each of the armed services had offices. I arrived at noon. The only recruiter not at lunch was a US Marine Corps Sergeant. He took full advantage of the situation and told me how great I'd look in Marine Corps dress blues. I said, "Sign me up." He did, and I left humming the Marine Corps Hymn. On July 1, 1960, I was on a train headed to boot camp at Parris Island, South Carolina, to begin my three-year hitch as a US Marine.

My first two years in the service were spent as a member of the Marine Corps Ceremonial Guard Company in Washington DC and then the Marine Corps Drill team. It was a different world, being a dressed up Marine. Duty was marching in parades, participating in veterans' funerals at the National Cemetery in Arlington, and being part of events around DC, including an occasional White House function. If I liked getting all dressed up and standing at attention, it would have been a good career choice. During my last year I was transferred to the Marine Corps base in Quantico, Virginia. I was part of the security detail for the US President's helicopter unit, Marine One. I traveled with the helicopters by aircraft carrier to Costa Rica. John F Kennedy spent a week there in conference with South American leaders and used the three choppers to get around Central America. I finished my service obligation just before marines were sent to Vietnam, so thankfully was never in a combat situation.

Guard duty is mostly boring. There's lots of time to think ... and think. I considered other careers, but finally realized that my ideal life might be as a large animal vet instead of farming. It was still about animals and the outdoors. As my three-year enlistment was winding down, I applied to and was accepted as an undergraduate at Cornell University in Ithaca, New York. I spent two years there taking the required courses to qualify for admission to the vet school. Because I was motivated I studied hard, and my grades were competitive enough to qualify. The final hurdle was an interview.

The interview was a conducted by a committee of five veterinary professors. They sat at a long table, two on each side, and the chairman at the end. At the other end of the table, there was an empty chair for the applicant. I showed up for the interview in the required coat and tie. It was very intimidating. Mrs. Roberts was secretary for the committee. She had a desk outside the interview room. Her job was to escort the applicant into the interview room and introduce everyone. I arrived 15 minutes early. Mrs. Roberts sat me down to wait. My nervousness must have been obvious, so she suggested that I go out in the hall and have a drink at the water fountain. The fountain was acting up that day. When I pushed the little button on top, a blast of water exploded from the outlet. I was soaked. My face, ironed white shirt and clip-on necktie were drenched. I went back in to see Mrs. Roberts and told her that I had just been attacked by the water fountain. She jumped up and said, "Well, you can't go in there looking like that!" which made me even more nervous. From somewhere she found a towel and started blotting my face and shirt front, saying all the while, "Oh no, we have to clean you up fast. They're almost done with the student ahead of you." The more frantically she patted me with the towel, the more nervous I got. The call came from the interview room, and she escorted me in. If anyone on the committee noticed my damp shirt, they were polite enough not to comment.

As I remember, they were kind to me, were curious about my Marine Corps experience, what my plans were for after vet school, and things like that. Remember, I was just two years out of the marines and still had a total respect for authority. Faced with all the officials, I barked out answers to their questions with a "Yes sir!", or "No sir!" and everything but, "Aye, aye sir!" Maybe that's why they let me in.

During my years in the service, I had started dating Bonnie, a high school classmate. I was in love, and whenever I had a long liberty weekend, I hitchhiked home from DC to New York to see her. After my acceptance at the vet school, we set a date and on June 12, 1965, were married. In September we drove to Ithaca, and I began the vet school experience.

\* \* \* \*

Afterthoughts by Dr Hunt:

Dave and I grew up only eleven miles away from each other in New York's Westchester County. He grew up in Pelham, which is in Eastern Westchester on Long Island Sound and, at age ten, I moved to Dobbs Ferry, which is across the county on the Hudson River. Our childhoods were very similar. Both of our fathers commuted into New York City, we grew up in small middle class suburbs, and we both loved the outdoors. For Dave, the outdoors meant farming, and for me, it meant ecology and the environment. That difference led us down different paths in veterinary medicine.

# Chapter 2
## Veterinary School

# Dr Hunt: Vet School Highlight Reel (Bloopers)

I was in vet school over 40 years ago and I still have a gut reaction thinking about it. I confess I had stress diarrhea the entire time I was in school. The amount of material we had to learn and the pressure of staying on top of everything was constant. There were about 100 of us in the class. Rather than competing against each other, we banded together to give each other strength, encouragement, and support. I still stay in touch with some of my classmates and one, Tom, is my best friend.

So, what was vet school like at Michigan State University? The MSU campus is one of the largest in the nation with over 40,000 students. It's like a small city. The Red Cedar River is lined with large trees and runs right through the older part of campus, which consists of two or three story red brick buildings with their original areas of study engraved in stone over the front doors, like forestry or entomology. Between classes the sidewalks are bustling with students scurrying to their next class. Five minutes later the campus could be deserted except for a few students sprinting to a class, haphazardly dressed, because they just woke up. The vet school was a relatively newer addition built on the southern part of campus that was formerly farmland. My walk to classes was relatively short because I lived in the newly built graduate student dorm nearby. My room was just large enough to have a bed, desk and chair. I felt like I was a monk in a cubicle at a seminary, except I had a large window facing a forest reserve at the edge of campus. In the winter after a snowfall it was a winter wonderland, and in October a burst of yellow and red painted my view. If not in class, I was either studying in my room or out for a run along the Red Cedar.

During the first year we learned the fundamentals of anatomy, physiology, nutrition, and immunology. The next year we focused on body systems like the respiratory, nervous, digestive, and musculoskeletal systems, as well as pharmacology, surgery, and diagnostics. We had to learn all the unique characteristics of dogs, cats, horses, cows, sheep, pigs, and exotic animals. Our final year was made up of two-week rotations where we were split up into small groups to focus on areas of veterinary medicine like surgery, ophthalmology, neurology, farm calls, and equine medicine. The rotations were an opportunity to apply what we learned in class with real life cases. Each rotation was like opening the prize in a Cracker Jack box, you didn't know what to expect. Each professor had his or her way of putting you through the rigors that are part of vet medicine. Whoever you got, you were expected to know your stuff and perform like you were a veterinarian. More on that later.

One common feature of all the rotations was the "hurry up and wait" way of doing things. As seniors we were the grunts, so to speak. The MSU vet school was a practicing vet facility with real-life clients, so the faculty was ultimately responsible for getting the job done. We were a teaching hospital, which meant the seniors did all the running around and taking the patients to various parts of the hospital to do tests. Inherently this was a very inefficient way of doing things. It was routine for me to be told to rush a dog down to the radiology department and get an x-ray as soon as possible. When I got down there, I checked in with a classmate doing her radiology rotation, then proceeded to fall into a long line of other classmates with pets from other departments who were told to rush down to the radiology department and get an x-ray as soon as possible. As much as I bitched and moaned, though, I actually enjoyed vet school.

There were plenty of fun times during vet school. One of our classmates, Sam, was a former cheerleader for MSU. If we were in a funk, which was a regular occurrence, he would get up in front of the class before lecture and begin to yell out a cheer while performing the acrobatic stunts he did at football games. Hacky Sack was becoming popular on campus, and Tom and I would study together and take Hacky Sack breaks (or rather we would take study breaks between Hacky Sack). Tom thought it would be a good idea to bring it to our tedious pharmacology lectures. We would sneak out of lecture and play under the stairwells in the building. This did not go unnoticed by our classmates. Eventually we had 12 people in a circle under the stairwell knocking around the Hacky Sack during lecture. The reason we all felt safe skipping a lecture was because the class banded together to form a rotating lecture note taking scheme. Each student was assigned a lecture for which he or she was responsible for taking notes, printing them out and passing them out to the rest of the class. This plan was a double edged sword, though. The nice thing was if you missed a class for whatever reason, like if you were in the hospital with a deadly disease (or playing Hacky Sack in the hallway), you knew you were getting the notes. The bad part of this plan was every student had their own way of note taking: some very detailed, some lacking any details, others unorganized or full of abbreviations only the note taker knew. I tried not to miss class unless I knew who was taking notes that day. Our Hacky Sack skips were well planned.

Sports helped relieve stress. I loved to play racquetball. One Saturday morning, I invited one of my classmates to play. Lew was six-foot four-inches, with an arm span of a Condor. All he had to do was stand in the middle of the court to reach most of my shots, so my strategy was to tucker him out. Taking advantage of my endurance from being a distance runner, I started peppering balls to the side walls so he had to run over to get them. After the first game, during which he creamed me, I got him so tired he couldn't move any more. Revenge is sweet.

We also had an intramural basketball team. Big Lew was our center. Pete was small and quick, so he handled the ball. Tom, Ken, Chris, and I ran around trying to get free. I don't remember any one of us acting as a coach or captain. It was a democratic effort. It had to be because veterinary students tend to be driven, focused, serious students. Somehow it worked. Our friendship and respect for each other made it work. And besides, we were strictly mediocre and we weren't out there to claim the Intramural Crown. The younger undergraduate teams handed us our asses most of the time, but we had fun and it was a rare time we were together outside of class not studying.

Lectures were an interesting study of student psychology. There were always the kids that sat up front—the diligent note takers. There was a classmate that always had a can of Diet Coke on her desk. Others had food they would pull out of their backpacks. My classmates that grew up on farms had empty Styrofoam coffee cups on their desks so they could spit their chewing tobacco into them. Tom and I always sat in the very back. We wanted to stay under the radar. God forbid we were called on to answer a question. The front row kids typically shot their hands up, unknowingly saving Tom and my butts. I have a gripe about my classmate and friend Tom. Exams were intense. I would agonize over every question. Tom is an impatient guy. His impatience got the better of him during exams. After about 15 minutes you could hear him sigh and he would start rifling through the exam, marking answers in an irritating, frantic manner, and then he would walk out of the exam halfway through—and darn it if he didn't get a B or A on the exam. I secretly hated him for it in a respectful, fond way. As it turned out the professors made sure we were all on the same level. They made us all look stupid. Some profs did it on purpose, but most were simply trying to teach us so much in so little time.

There was an equine professor that had a bad reputation among the non-equine oriented students. Dr Branch was large, loud, demanding, and a stickler for detail. He was hard on the students and would berate them in front of clients. I was petrified that I would get him for my equine rotation. My GI tract went into overdrive in anticipation. But to be fair my equine-focused classmates thought he was great and not a bad guy once you got to know him. I didn't want to find out. Fortunately, I got Dr Snow, the nicest, calmest, most understanding equine prof in school. I think he knew I was a small animal guy. But I still messed up. A classmate and I were charged with taking the daily temperature of a rather large horse (all horses were large to me at the time). We were taught to tie the rectal thermometer to a clamp with a string so we could clip the thermometer to the horse's tail to avoid losing it. With my classmate holding the horse steady, I inserted the thermometer, but before I could clip it to the tail the horse swung its hips to the side and pushed me away. The thermometer disappeared. Was it inside the horse? Was it in the straw bedding? For a second we stood there in petrified panic. We didn't want to do a rectal exam. We hadn't learned how to yet. Telling our professor was out of the question. Our only recourse was to look in the straw. This was worse than finding a needle in a haystack. We had a 600-pound horse that was already pissed at us for interrupting her peaceful morning. We were on our hands and knees combing the straw while the horse was nervously dancing around us. On top of that I couldn't breathe because I was wheezing from my hay allergy. Luck was on our side, though, and we eventually found it before our prof stopped by to see how we were doing.

On one of my farm call rotations, we came upon a farm with a farrowing pig in dystocia. Four stone-faced students stood circling the pig that was on its side in distress trying to give birth. The vet suggested someone should do a vaginal exam to see if a piglet was stuck. "Any volunteers?" he asked. All four of us stood motionless, looking down at the pig as if we were thinking veterinary things with our hands tucked firmly in our pockets. "Ok, Hunt, go in," he said to me. "Why me?" I said to myself, "I thought I was here just to observe?" As if reading my mind, the prof said, "Hunt, you have the smallest hands, so you should be able to get in there." So I got down onto my stomach on the barn floor and examined the sow while trying to describe what I felt. My overalls smelled like pig shit the rest of the day. No one wanted to sit next to me in the farm call truck.

Another pig story: I was volunteered to draw blood from a research pig at the MSU vet school—a large pig that seemed 2000 pounds when I first saw it. I grabbed an unwilling classmate to hold the snout ring (the ring acts as a restraining device and forces the chin up) so I could stick a four inch needle into the neck to draw the blood. First of all, I had to find the jugular vein in the neck that is all fat. Secondly, I had to find it quickly because the pig let out the loudest, most irritating squeal right in my face. The longer it took me to find the vein, the longer it squealed. The longer it squealed, the less likely I would find the jugular. I had to do this every day for seven days. But do you know what? I love bacon. Tasty revenge.

Our junior year we had small animal surgery labs. The instructor was a prissy, picky Brit named Dr Wallace—not a warm and fuzzy kind of guy. Four students were assigned a dog to anesthetize and then we would perform basic surgery. Don't worry, these dogs had a life at MSU that was 100 times better than the pound. Dr Wallace would walk from one table to the next, looking at the work being done, and many times would grab scissors and remove the stitches a student just spent 15 minutes installing, saying it was wrong. "Do it again," he would say. I must admit he taught good technique. The surgery room technician ran the place. He was an ex-army medic in his 50s who looked and acted like a drill sergeant. If you didn't scrub in properly, he told you in no uncertain terms. We were all scared, respectful and fond of him all at the same time. One of my classmates, Paul, was the son of a world-renowned veterinary surgeon. Paul was a teacher turned veterinarian. He was in his mid-30s by the time he came to vet school. He was also about six-foot two inches. During our first surgery all of us were standing around a surgery table with our dog, dressed in our surgery gowns, hats, masks, and gloves under a hot surgery light. We were listening to *the Sargeant* bark at us, when all of a sudden I saw Paul crumble to the ground in a dead faint. We never let him forget that one.

In my orthopedic rotation I had to present a hip surgery technique to the orthopedic instructor and some of my classmates. I went step by step and thought I did a good job. When I finished, the instructor asked the rest of the class, "So what is wrong with Hunt's technique?" No one could answer because they all thought it was correct. Finally, he said, "It's the wrong approach. That was the anterior approach. I wanted the posterior approach." I got a pass from my classmates and the instructor had the slightest sympathetic smirk on his face.

Sometimes professors surprise you. My neurology professor and I would have conversations about animal behavior. One hot topic in those days was dominance aggression in dogs. He felt it was a genetic neurologic driven behavior, and I thought it had a learned component and could be controlled through behavior modification. One day he asked me to go with him to a lecture he was giving on dominance aggression to the Springer Spaniel Breeders Club. Springers seem to be over represented in dominance aggression cases. He would give the neurological side of the problem and I would give the behavioral side. While preparing, I felt I was reenacting the scene in the movie *The Paper Chase*, where Hart, the law student, spent the entire weekend hardly sleeping, writing a brief for Professor Kinsfield, his contracts law professor. Unlike Hart, I got it done and went to the lecture with my professor. I felt pretty special that evening.

In my large animal surgery class, my surgery group was assigned a donkey. She had quite the personality—very sweet, agreeable, and tolerant of our shenanigans. At the end of the term, the head technician, who grew very fond of our group, adopted her and took her home. We were so happy to know that our surgery patient went to a good home. Our surgery labs were in the afternoon. Dr A, our surgery instructor, would make a bag of microwave popcorn several hours into the lab. The smell of fresh popcorn wafted into the lab from his office. He would walk around the lab eating his popcorn out of the bag. We were all pretty hungry by then and the popcorn drove us crazy and Dr A knew it. He would take a kernel and wedge it under our surgery masks. To keep sterility we couldn't touch our masks, so we had to contort our faces to try and maneuver the popcorn into our mouths. Dr A took delight in watching our surgery masks twist and turn as we desperately tried to snag the popcorn.

    I was not an A student. I was my own worst enemy during a test, second guessing myself, not reading the question right, or misreading the multiple choice answers. But I can brag about one academic achievement. In our senior year we were prepped to qualify to be a Certified Federal Veterinary Agent. We had to pass an exam at the end of training. I got a 100% on the test. No one else in my class got a perfect score. Not even the brainy young hot shots! I bet my classmates were as surprised as I was. For that brief moment I imagined my classmates thinking, *Gee, Hunt really is smart. Who would have known?* or, *Hunt must have cheated!*

    All the vet school instructors were dedicated to giving us a good education—they just had different ways of doing it. I had a huge crush on one faculty member. She was about my age, beautiful and light hearted. If I had the chance, I would have followed her around like a puppy dog. But the faculty member that I remember the most was a surgeon, Dr F. She was an outstanding teacher because she kept things uncomplicated and had a "you can do this" attitude with the students. What stood out the most for me was that she respected me. She saw me as a potentially capable, talented veterinarian and treated me as such even though I wasn't at the time. I had an immediate respect and admiration for her. As a student assistant in surgery, she treated me like a colleague, and when I saw her in the hallway, she always greeted me by name. That blew me away. I used her surgery techniques textbook throughout my career and still have it on my bookshelf. Some instructors did have a sense of humor. Our neurology professor used to whistle the song, "If I only Had

A Brain" from *The Wizard of Oz* during exams.

Field Trips—remember those in grade school? They were such a big deal. Permission slips, special packed lunch or lunch money, your good clothes. We had field trips in vet school, but they were a little different. In those days drug companies were flush with cash for promoting their products. They wanted their name in our heads before graduating. UpJohn had a major facility in Kellogg, Michigan, about an hour and a half from MSU. They invited our class to tour the manufacturing facility and brainwash us. We didn't mind. It was a day off from classes, and they provided a nice bus and a good lunch. As we were getting on the bus to go back to MSU, the UpJohn rep pulled a wad of cash from his pocket and offered to supply the bus with food and drink for the ride home. We politely accepted the offer, trying to hide our excitement for this good fortune. So, we had a party. The bus driver was the only one left sober by the end of the trip. Junk food was passed around, and the booze was flowing like a river during a spring melt. We were singing, shouting, and playing games. Our yearbook has a picture of me on the losing end of a strip poker game. I looked pretty happy for losing. Once again, my classmates saw another side of me, "Hunt is not only smart (sometimes) but he is a party animal (rarely)."

At graduation I was selected by the class to receive the Student Appreciation Award. I think it was because I managed to get a fantastic moneymaking gig for the class. During football season on the Sunday following a home game, the university hired our class to clean the stadium. Now, MSU is a Big Ten University with a big football program and an even bigger football stadium that holds a gazillion people. During home games as I was walking past the stadium on my way to the library I could feel the roar of the crowd inside this Roman-style coliseum. Well, MSU paid us $500 per game, for four games, to go in and pick up all the trash left behind. With the entire class joining in we got through in about two hours. I have never seen so many Peppermint Schnapps bottles in my life. It was probably the easiest $2000 any of us made, even as vets!

These are some of the memorable highlights of vet school. Most of the time we were studying our asses off, trying to survive in a very rigorous, intense, unrelenting program. When I see Doctorate of

Veterinary Medicine after my name, I think of two things—how proud I am to have earned that degree and how I disproved the notion that I was not smart enough to get a doctorate. Revenge is gratifying.

I would never do it again, though, and my intestinal tract thanks me for that.

\* \* \* \*

Afterthoughts by Dr Jefferson:

This was fun to read, and so totally different from my own experience. In the end we were exposed to and learned the same things, but getting there was not at all the same. I didn't play any sports or do anything extracurricular during my vet training at Cornell. I never once even kicked a hacky sack. Now that I'm retired I'll have to ask John to show me how to do that. At Cornell, in my time, the administration would have called out the hacky sack police. Kicking a leather ball around under the stairway instead of attending a lecture? I can't believe that John's professor didn't notice that a good percentage of his class was missing, but just kept droning on. At Cornell they took attendance at each class. Miss a class twice and it would have been a summons to see the dean. For sure we didn't have as much fun. Anyway, for both of us, vet school was no walk in the park. We should have considered plant biology. I think all you have to know is up the xylem and down the phloem.

# Dr Jefferson: Four Years at Cornell Vet School

As I mentioned in the last chapter, Bonnie and I were married a few months before my first semester of vet school started. Married life in college is not like the life of a single student. We moved in different circles, and our priorities were different. Bonnie took a job teaching second grade in a local school. She also was working toward her master's degree which involved an hour long evening commute to Cortland. She returned late and sometimes found me asleep over a textbook. Full days for us both!

There were only a few married students in my class. In addition, I was one of the oldest students in the class, having been in the military for three years. As a result most of the people we hung around with were teachers that Bonnie knew. They supported their spouses who were in graduate programs at Cornell. What we all had in common was a severe lack of disposable income. It was the mid-1960s but still, Bonnie's salary at $3200 per year meant a lot of penny pitching. By careful shopping we kept our grocery bills down to $10 a week.

Every day I took a sandwich and a cookie to school. The sandwich was in a baggie, and both it and my cookie were in a paper bag. We were so frugal that I would bring the baggie and the paper bag home every night to get several trips out of them. I had my tuition and some school expenses paid by the GI bill, so we graduated with virtually no debt. The average load today for a graduating vet is $180,000. The last vet I hired was $300,000 in debt on graduation day. Such a burden!

The specter of flunking out and not becoming a vet and a good provider kept me studying whenever I wasn't in class. I was running scared. It wasn't until halfway through my third year that the fear of not making it all the way to graduation finally left me.

We lived in an apartment house in Ithaca our first two years. The rent was reasonable, but the place was not kept up. The owner was a businessman in downtown Ithaca. One day, I was annoyed enough to drive down to see him and complain about the building's condition. On the spot he hired me to take over the maintenance. We negotiated a decrease in our rent in exchange for me keeping the hallways swept, shoveling the snow, and mowing the lawn.

In my third year I heard about a completely rent-free option a 20 minute walk from the vet school. That apartment took up the third floor of a large house. The two of us rattled around in six big rooms. The house was next to, and owned by, the Lutheran church. It was a sweet deal that had been passed down within the vet school for years. We didn't pay any rent in exchange for my taking on the job of church sexton. The term is from colonial America where the sexton was the church property caretaker and grave digger. In today's language I was the janitor. Grave digging was not one of my duties.

Our son, Jim, was born halfway through my senior year. He was three months premature, so it made for a rough start. Bonnie stopped working to be a full-time mom. We lived the rest of the senior year on money that we saved from the year before. Looking back that seems impossible, but we did it.

There was so much to cover in veterinary school that there were no breaks during the day. It was 8 a.m. to 4 p.m. straight classes or labs. Sometimes we'd sit in the same lecture room for four hours straight, and the professors would be the ones who moved around. It makes me twitch just remembering that. The first year anatomy course had a dissection lab that was four hours long, five days a week. Each lecture meant more information to absorb and then learn. You really had to hit the books every night just to keep up. You couldn't flunk a subject because all the courses were sequential, and today's information built on what you learned yesterday. I found the mathematics of probability in genetics difficult, and still, 50 years later, have nightmares about those courses and their exams.

The class I enjoyed the most was large animal restraint. At that time tranquilizers and anesthetics weren't as sophisticated as today, so we learned how to use ropes to pull horses and cows down and tie them up for procedures. That class was held outside in a grassy paddock. The school horses got so used to this that a couple of them would just lay down when the ropes came out. The knots and rope procedures I learned came in handy all through my career. I understand this course no longer exists, but it was fun for us.

Despite my lack of interest in small animals, I got good grades in those courses. That's because I didn't have any firsthand experience. When it came time for exams, I sat down and memorized, for example, the ten signs of distemper. Most everyone else in the class had lots of small animal experience and had seen distemper first hand, so they could wing it and get six signs right without cracking a book. Not me, I had to learn all ten because I didn't have that small animal experience. Again, I was running scared.

The senior year was mostly spent in clinics. There was a small animal clinic, a large animal clinic, and the ambulatory service (on the road seeing animals on nearby farms). I liked the large animal and the ambulatory sections. I didn't like the small animal hospital. I just couldn't relate.

Lots of x-rays were taken in both the small and large animal clinics. At the time the x-rays for both the small and the large animal hospitals were run through a processor which was located near the large animal clinic. It's not like today where all the images are electronically generated and instantly available. In the small animal clinic, when a dog or cat was x-rayed, the films had to be taken down two hallways to the processor. I always volunteered to go so that I could stop in for 20 minutes to see what was going on with the horses in the hospital. I don't think the doctors in the small animal hospital ever learned my name as I would duck out as often as I could. If they asked what took so long, I would say, "Big line to use the processor."

Before one even applies to vet school there have been countless quizzes and examinations in the courses leading to a bachelor's degree. It starts all over again in vet school with four more years of classes and even more exams. You would think that after all the testing, taking yet another exam in vet school would be old hat. It was never old hat, especially in the junior year. The most dreaded exam was in Dr Delahanty's large animal surgery course. Dr D, as he preferred to be called, was a 5 foot 6 inch scrappy Irishman with a grin that took up the whole lower half of his face. He shaved his head once a week, which at the time was unusual. He was a showman in everything he did. Dr D didn't like writing exams or grading them. His final exam was oral. We knew from last year's class what to expect.

## Dog and Pony Show

Here is how it worked. You signed up for an appointment time for your final exam in his office. It was just him and you and a Ping-Pong ball raffle cage. It was a round wire cage about the size of a volley ball. It was sitting on his desk when I walked into his office. It was half full of Ping-Pong balls, each with a number on them. Dr D said, "Jefferson, you've heard about my little machine."

"Yes, sir, I have."

"I'd like to review the rules. You don't mind?"

"No, sir, I'd appreciate it."

"OK. You turn the crank to get the balls all mixed up. When it stops, open the little trap door, reach in and grab a ball. You show it to me. I have in front of me a list of 59 questions. As you know there are 60 students in your class. I take the number you pulled and read off that question on my sheet. You have 15 minutes to give me a complete answer. I may give you a hint to jog your memory; otherwise it's your show. If you get the ball without a number, you have a choice. You can take a chance and maybe improve your grade by spinning again, or you can say, 'I'm fine'. In that case we go to the lunch room, I buy you a coffee, and you accept the grade you have going in. Is that clear?"

"Yes, sir."

I can't begin to tell you how apprehensive I was. The word apprehensive has a Greek root. Roughly translated it means, "scared to death." Turning the crank made the balls a blur of white. It sounded like a popcorn machine. I let go of the crank, and the balls settled down. I reached in and pulled one off the top of the pile. It said 38.

Dr D looked down at his list of questions. "Mmmm, not an easy one. Describe the descent of the testicles in our domestic large animal species." I understood the question. In each of these animals such as horse, cow, pig, goat, and sheep, testicles descend from inside the body cavity to move down a canal into the scrotum. The descent time varies with the type of animal. It can happen during the pregnancy or at some time after birth. So, I understood the question but had no idea what the answer was. Remember, in vet school you can't flunk a course. They build on each other. Flunk a course, and until you pass it, your education is on hold. All that ran through my head.

"Dr D, I have no idea."

He looked at me a long minute, letting me dangle there, and then said, "OK, let's reason through this. Tell me what you know about testicular descent in horses."

"Well, during pregnancy the testicles follow a tract down into the scrotum and generally, unless they are retained within the body, the colt is born with the testicles in the scrotum."

"OK. What happens if they stay inside the body and don't descend?"

I also knew that. "If they are both retained, we call the colt a cryptorchid which means hidden testicle. If just one is in the scrotum, and the other is retained, the animal is called a monorchid. If neither descends into the scrotum, the body heat kills the sperm, and the horse is sterile."

"And," Dr D asked, "although sterile, will they still act like a stud?"

I answered, "Yes, they will. The heat of the body kills the sperm, but the testosterone is still produced, so he will act like a stallion and breed mares, but will not become a father."

Dr D led me through the subject for the full 15 minute appointment, and when it was over, I realized that my working knowledge of the subject was OK. I was almost starting to enjoy the conversation. I learned that in the hands of someone who cares about his students, a skillful conversation will reveal whether the student knows his or her stuff.

Fifty years later I am teaching large animal medicine at a local community college to vet tech students. As I look over my room of students taking one of my exams, I remember my 15 minutes with Dr D. I'm looking for the blank stare, the cold sweat, or even some telltale restlessness. It hasn't happened yet, but when it does, I will walk by the student and drop a note on her desk. It will ask her to follow me out to the hallway. Out there I'll shut the door and tell her that she seems a little nervous. "Which question are you having trouble with?" We'll talk about the question and how to think about it. Soon I'll know whether or not she knows the material. If she knows it, she'll be assured that she won't flunk. I'll invite her to go back in and give it her best shot. What more could we ask anyway? In a few days she'll forget the question and the exam, but my hope is that she'll remember the coaching just as I remembered Dr D's. The best outcome would be that they will do the same for someone who is on the spot and just needs someone who is paying attention.

In my years at Cornell vet school the administration only allowed two female students per year. Believe it or not, our class had none. So, when a professor entered our class and saw that it was all male, we sometimes heard the comment, "Well, looks like I can finally tell some dirty jokes." It wasn't that there weren't female applicants for the seats. The theory was that the seats should be reserved for men. It was believed that women would marry soon after graduation, leave the profession, and become stay-at-home moms. It was thought that it would have been a wasted education that some man could have had. How times changed! Today over 90% of the entering students at every vet school are women, and the profession now reflects that. In the course of my career I hired seven associate vets, five of whom were women. All were bright and capable. Most did get married and kept right on practicing, so I guess the old theory was flawed.

*  *  *  *

Afterthoughts by Dr Hunt:

Dave went to vet school about ten years before me, and social changes were afoot during that decade. When I arrived in vet school in 1979, the average age of the class was around 25, a number of students were married, and 40% of the class were women, so Dave would have fit in more comfortably in my class demographic. My married classmates had domestic responsibilities that I didn't have to think about. Balancing studying and family obligations must have been incredibly difficult. I got to know many of my classmates' spouses, and they were unbelievably supportive and understanding of how suffocating vet school could be. I had the utmost respect and fondness for them. Dave's chapter gives you a glimpse of married life in vet school and Bonnie's role in helping him through.

Dave's story about the horses automatically lying down when they saw the students with ropes is charming. The lifelong lesson he learned from the professor was far more influential than memorizing the name of some tiny artery in a cow's leg. Dave, staying under the radar in small animal classes, was identical to me remaining anonymous in large animal classes.

# Chapter 3
## Getting a Job

## Dr Hunt: The Interviews

The last term in veterinary school was a head spinner. We were finishing up two-week rotations in specific areas of veterinary medicine like radiology, surgery, or dermatology. These rotations were intense and stressful, we were also studying for the National and State Boards, and, oh yeah, we had to find a job! The majority of my classmates were looking for jobs in Michigan near their homes. Others were flying out West to California or Colorado, and some of us from New England were setting our sights back East.

My intentions were always to return to New England. I researched job opportunities in the American Veterinary Medical Association journal and on the jobs board at school. The Internet was not yet invented. Reading job openings became an art. They all used the same phrases to describe their practice: "busy small animal practice with good clientele," "near mountains and seacoast," "looking for hard working, energetic candidates," "equipped with x-ray and full surgery." What was not said was just as important, though. Salaries and long term futures at the practices were rarely advertised. Another subtlety I discovered was how old the advertisement was or how often the practice re-advertised the same position. A long running ad could mean no one wanted the job or the owner was super picky. A repeating ad may have meant that the practice was a revolving door: taking in new grads, working them to death, then spitting them out and replacing them with another low salaried new graduate. I really didn't appreciate all the hidden messages until I was looking for new jobs later in my career. As a senior, wholly ignorant of the real world, I ignored all the hidden warnings and proceeded to select almost every job opening from New Jersey up to Maine. Little did I know I was about to get an education in job searching that vet school never taught me.

A month before graduation, my fiancé and I flew home to New York to start the interview quest. I borrowed my dad's retired, antiquated VW Squareback. I was counting on it to get me to 17 interviews up and down the East Coast. We almost didn't make it! It was an ugly tan with rust eating away at the rocker panels and cancerous looking spots scattered over the body. The wipers smeared instead of wiped, and going up hills was interminable. I was a VW fan like Dad, though. I overlooked the old Squareback's shortcomings. That was a mistake.

My first interview was in an industrial town in New Jersey. The day was overcast and cool, making the city look even more depressing. After a tour of the clinic, the owner sat us down in his office with a pad of paper in hand. He wrote something down and asked me, "How much do you think I should pay you?" I was taken aback. I didn't know what to say. I figured, as the owner, he would have a handle on what he could afford, how much revenue a new associate could generate, etc. I couldn't answer at first. He persisted. I was like a deer in the headlights. I can't remember the number, but I mumbled something in the range my classmates told me new grads were getting. He said that was about right. I wanted to leave ASAP. Right then and there I decided to cross this guy off the list. If he played games with me on a salary, what kind of shenanigans would he play at work?

I had several interviews in New Hampshire. When I arrived at one small-town practice, the vet was in the middle of pulling porcupine quills out of a dog's snout. He was understandably distracted during my visit. I didn't need a tour because I could see the entire facility while standing near the surgery table. The dog had a syringe filled with anesthetic taped to its front leg. The vet was using a short-acting barbiturate typically used to induce dogs for surgery. That wasn't what we were taught in school. He had to keep injecting small amounts to keep the dog asleep as he yanked one quill at a time. I was appalled. Little did I know that quill pulling was going to be a common feature at my practice in Bucksport and I would be doing the same thing.

At another interview I walked into a converted garage, which was one large room with a surgery table in the back. That is where I found my next potential future boss—until I saw him perform surgery. After gloving up for a surgery, he would handle non-sterile objects and adjust the anesthetic machine with his gloves on and then return to surgery. That was an immediate reject. I never did that in the 33 years I practiced medicine.

*Dog and Pony Show*

    Car troubles began the third day into our journey after driving in heavy rain on Interstate 95 in Connecticut. While driving through Massachusetts on Route 495 near Hudson, the car started to lose power. It wasn't responding to the accelerator. I would floor it and it would just keep puttering at 50 mph and was getting slower by the minute. And I wasn't even going up a hill. Fortunately, I found an exit and barely made it to a gas station before the car stopped running like it was too tired to go any further. The mechanic found a lot of water in the gas tank. Apparently, the gas feed from the cap to the tank was exposed in the wheel well, an obvious design flaw. It rusted out and allowed water in from the tires when it rained. The good news was that there was a nice hotel across the street.

    Eventually we arrived at a modern vet practice in southern New Hampshire. It was a clean, bright, well laid out hospital owned by a serious doctor with extremely specific ideas on how to run the clinic. He was a little intimidating, but that didn't bother me so much as the fact that his wife was the general manager. That raised yellow flags for me as a future associate or employee. In those days many spouses, out of economic necessity, helped manage the practice, and I am sure they all did a great job. It was the conflict of interest or prejudiced loyalty I had to deal with as an employee that bothered me. It didn't sit well. While practicing in Connecticut, I worked for a practice where the vet's wife was the manager, and it turns out my fears were well founded. The staff was always at war with the wife, and her managing style was disrespectful and always sided with her husband. After a while the staff started coming to me for guidance and decisions. I sympathized with their grievances but couldn't help them; I was an employee like them. I vowed then and there that there would be no relatives in my own practice.

    In Kennebunk, Maine I interviewed at a huge, gorgeous new vet facility. There were multiple exam rooms, large surgery suites, and a big lab. The owner was an elderly, tall, gray haired vet that was soft spoken and fatherly. He seemed tired, and the facility was way too large for him to handle. We hit it off immediately. I didn't realize at the time, but he tested me by having me look at a fecal sample to diagnose Giardia. I guess I passed the test because he not only offered me a job but also offered me the practice too. If I only knew then what I know now—I should have taken it. But I was too scared, too unsure of myself, and knew nothing of running a business. Vet school neglected to teach us how to run a business.

Another new facility I visited was in Bangor, Maine. At the time, Bangor seemed like a frontier outpost on the edge of a vast uninhabited primitive pine forest. Car trouble haunted us again. We arrived in Bangor in the evening and we were already late for the interview. The gas gauge was pointing to E. In my experience there is always a gallon or two left when on E. I thought I could get to the interview first and then get gas, but the VW Squareback had other ideas. We ran out of gas about two miles from the clinic. I had to call the vet to drive me to the nearest gas station. He was very gracious and understanding. In my mind I blew it. He did offer me a job, but I didn't like the ten minute office call schedule and assembly line nature. I also wanted to be closer to family at the time. Years later I set up shop for 26 years in Bucksport, just down the Penobscot River from Bangor, the town I perceived earlier as a frontier outpost.

I was offered a job in all the practices I visited. I was even offered a job from a large animal vet from "The County", in northern Maine, during my state licensing exam. The one I settled on was in Avon, Connecticut. The hospital was a converted brick ranch house. The staff was nice, the facility a little cramped, but clean and efficient. The vet was in his 50s but clearly still very excited about veterinary medicine. He specialized in dermatology and was interested in my background in animal behavior. He was of German stock and believed in hard work and fair wages. What drew me to him was his enthusiasm for our profession. He wanted to practice good, up to date medicine. He turned out to be a good mentor for this insecure yet excited newbie.

When I owned my own practice, I interviewed potential associates and it wasn't easy. The truth is an interview rarely gives you a true picture of the candidate. Several vets I hired turned out to be kind of crazy or irresponsible or both, so I wonder what the vets were thinking when they interviewed me. I bet the bar was set low: upright and breathing.

*Dog and Pony Show*

\* \* \* \*

Afterthoughts by Dr Jefferson:

We get so pumped up before an interview, and really, we learn so little from them. Both sides are trying to say what we think the other party wants to hear. In that atmosphere honest feelings and opinions are held back. We have both learned that the best interview happens when prospective employees come and spend the day. As we see cases together and talk about approaches and opinions, communication is happening. I hired one vet on a recommendation, without her spending any time with us. That turned out not to be a good fit, for her or the practice. After that experience, I always required at least one full day with the practice as an interview. It became standard procedure for both vets and vet techs. You can only hold back who you really are for so long. That is so tiring. Given enough time, eventually you get real.

## Dr Jefferson: The Job Offer

The spring of 1969 was an exciting time for us seniors at the Cornell Vet School. Practicing veterinarians looking for a new graduate came to Cornell on a week in the early spring. Soon to be graduates looking for a job filled out a form that could have been titled, "My Perfect Job." Vets looking to hire filled out one that might have said, "My Perfect Candidate." The school had a sign in board for the vets and the students. The meetings were held in a quiet corner of the library, in the coffee shop, or sometimes in a donated professor's office.

I thought my perfect job at the time would be in a practice specializing in dairy cattle. If there was some horse work, fine, but I mostly wanted to work with cows. If there was some small animal work in the practice, I made it clear that it was not my strength or interest. Typically the interviews lasted about 30 minutes. The vet looking for help would describe the practice and their expectations. The candidate would tell the vet what they were looking for. Toward the end of the interview the money details came up.

"This is what we are offering and can afford to pay."

"This is what I need the first year."

Sometimes a vet would make an offer right then and there. Mostly they went home to look at their notes about the candidates, set them in order, and then would make an offer over the phone. I interviewed with a few large animal vets from the Northeast. I was taking notes on 3x5 cards during the interviews. When I was all done I had a handful of the cards with the vet's name, location, and any facts I remembered about the practice. The vets went back home to their busy lives, and we waited to hear from them. There was no internet then. The conversations were always by phone.

A week after the interviews I got a call from a man with a very deep voice. He gave his name. I didn't catch it.

"I was impressed that you've been in the service and that you are married. We are looking for someone who is mature and steady. I'm offering you a job, and want you to start right after graduation." The whole time he was talking I was frantically flipping through my cards because I had missed his name. I had absolutely no idea who I was talking to. None. I motioned to Bonnie, who was nearby. I put my hand over the speaker part of the phone and whispered,

"I think I am getting a job offer, but I have no idea who I'm talking to …"

Bonnie whispered, "Ask him how he spells his name."

I did.

The answer came back slowly and distinctly: "E…r…b".

I said, "Go on."

He said, "That's it. E…r…b. Dr Erb."

I dropped the deck of cards while fumbling through them. Bonnie and I scrambled around on the floor, looking to find the card that had his name on it. There, there it was: "Dr Erb, Landaff, New Hampshire. General practice, both large and small animal. Mostly dairy. Looking for help to start right after graduation."

"Well, OK. Thanks for considering me, Dr Erb. I'll talk it over with Bonnie and will call you back.

After graduation Bonnie and I packed a U-Haul truck with everything we owned and drove to Landaff, New Hampshire, and I went to work for Dr Fred Erb, spelled E…r…b.

\* \* \* \*

Afterthoughts by Dr Hunt:

Our chapters describing our job interviews show how different things were, and yet how things never change. Meeting a potential employer in the corner of the Cornell Vet School library must have been nerve wracking. That meeting space was definitely to the advantage of the employer. Dave didn't have an opportunity to see the practice, meet the staff, or get the feel of the work environment. Ten years later, vet school seniors were going out to the practice for an interview. That is why my chapter is longer than Dave's, because my process was an adventure. I bet today's seniors can get a job listing app on their phones and have their interviews via Zoom.

Dr John H. Hunt and Dr David A. Jefferson

We both had to deal with the salary game. I think that is inevitable and part of the process—like buying a car. Lots of dancing around a final figure.

Dr Erb's phone call is hilarious. I can see Dave now in an absolute panic, trying to get his future employer's name. Priceless.

# Chapter 4
## The Early Years

## Dr Hunt: Pretending To Be A Vet

When I received my diploma in East Lansing on a sunny hot day in June, I was expected to go out into the world and be a full-fledged, qualified, licensed veterinarian. On the one hand I thought, *I got this*. On the other hand I was scared to death. I got past my biggest fear of vet school—taking the National Boards. Now I had to actually be a veterinarian—one of the most trusted professions in the country.

School had taught me a new language of medical terms, surgery techniques, laboratory procedures, diseases, nutrition, and physiology, from cows to cats! Despite all that knowledge crammed in my head, I didn't even know how to treat a cat abscess or express a dog's anal glands, but my first boss hired me anyway. He must have seen something in me that told him I would not screw up too badly. I hoped he saw how personable and respectful I was with the staff and clients. I call myself a people vet. My forte was first getting to know my clients and then collaborating with them to keep their family pet healthy. My boss figured that while practicing medicine can be learned, dealing with people can't be taught.

I took my first job in Avon, Connecticut, because it was close to my parents in New York, and it was a well-run, progressive small animal practice. The owner left me to my own devices, but I knew he was always watching. Our office was up in the unfinished attic in the clinic among boxes of supplies and old equipment. It reminded me of the attic I used to hack around in back in Chicago as a kid. He put a small school desk behind his larger desk. I would go up into the attic and sit at my desk pretending to do something, But I had nothing to do except look through my text books about a case I was working on. But my boss would be busy at his big desk doing paperwork necessary to run the business. Which he never shared with me. In those days new graduates learned to run a business when they finally had their own hospital. I would also see him reading my entries on patient cards from the day before. My heart would skip a beat when he lingered on a record. Was he going to turn around and say, "John, you handled the case all wrong?" He never did, but I was always on high screech, emotionally, when he and I were in the office together. He always had my back, though. He would not hesitate to come to the rescue if I was having trouble with a client. Oddly, he never interfered if I was having trouble with a surgery. There were a few surgeries that went sideways, but while I was sweating bullets trying to correct my mistake, he would stay in the attic. Looking back on it I can see his reasoning. You learn best when solving your own problems, although I didn't think that at the time.

Coming into a well-established, one-man practice was hard on my ego. No one wanted to see the *new guy*. They all wanted the *old guy*, and for good reason. Their choices were familiarity and experience, or me, a young pup wearing a too-large lab coat and a nervous and unsure demeanor. During a physical exam I would spend a very long time listening to the pet's heartbeat. I needed the time to wait for my own heart to calm down so I could hear the pet's heartbeat, and it didn't take me long to discover I could use the stethoscope as a delay tactic. The stethoscope in my ears was like a "Do Not Disturb" sign. (see photo on page 196) I stared off in the distance, hoping the client would leave me alone long enough for me to figure out what was wrong with their dog. It probably looked odd that I was listening to the heart when the presenting complaint was a lame leg. Some clients actually started talking to me. I would begin my auscultation and out of the corner of my eye I would see the owner's mouth moving. The "Do Not Disturb" message needed punctuation. I would take out one ear plug and say, "I'm sorry I can't hear you." The client would be very apologetic and stop talking. I would then return to my frantic search for a diagnosis and treatment.

The staff would give me new clients so I wouldn't have to be compared to my boss. He didn't mind. He actually encouraged it because that would grow his practice and allow him to take time off. The first vacation he took after I started was not what I was expecting. I figured he would take a week off and work on his gentleman farm nearby. Nope, he went to a major conference for ten days in Hawaii. I was a nervous wreck. I graduated in June and he was leaving in September. I was just figuring out cat abscesses, and my spay time was still in the 60 minute range, which, by the way, is horrible.

This is when the vet techs came into play. In vet school the techs were the bosses of the students. They said jump and we asked how high. But the vet techs at Avon were my saviors. They knew their job and knew what my job was supposed to be without overstepping their job description. They gave me generous time between office calls. They knew I was struggling, and I appreciated their sensitivity. I was my own worst enemy. While my boss was 3000 miles away sipping umbrella drinks on a beautiful sand beach (I mean, attending meetings), I was left holding the bag for every case that walked through the door. I had no experience, no cell phones, no computers, no internet. Just my text books up in the attic. My strategy for some cases was to develop a rule-out list that included every conceivable disease I could think of. My most memorable example was a black Labrador Retriever with a soft bump under the skin on the hip. This poor client must have left the clinic with her head spinning and totally confused. I was so nervous that I became a Chatty Cathy doll spewing out all the possibilities that I remembered from school, ranging from an abscess to a rare parasite seen only in Australia. I poked it, measured it, aspirated it, and would have done an MRI if I had the opportunity. An x-ray came to mind, but the owner looked like she'd had enough. After the office visit I had a chance to look at the aspirate to see globules of fat. It was a lipoma, a very common benign fatty tumor. When I called the owner I was more relieved than she was. Somehow, I made it through the ten days without getting sued. My techs saved my butt every day. I never forgot their help. I carried that respect for vet techs throughout my career, especially when I owned my own practice. Now I teach vet tech students, and I pepper my lectures with, "You guys are the most important part of the practice."

With time and practice my skills developed. I was unofficially assigned to put in all the catheters and IV lines in sick patients. I got pretty good at venipuncture and catheter placement, which can be tricky in pets that are old, dehydrated, or small. That served me well for the rest of my career. One weekend I had six IV's running simultaneously. Clogged catheters, twisted IV lines, empty fluid bottles, drip rate changes, and chewed lines were the common problems that came up. I felt like I was the plate spinning guy on the Ed Sullivan Show.

My clients were wonderful. I vetted for some famous people, like Katherine Hepburn's niece, who was an actress herself. But I also had some clients who were, shall I say, half a bubble off center. I had one client who loved her cat, but she seemed odd. Her clothes were mismatched and looked like they randomly came off the racks at Goodwill. During one visit I noticed she had a very red ear that looked infected. Then my eyes caught something on the back of her head. It was a large hair curler. It was all I could do not to stare at the roller. I felt so bad. I didn't want to embarrass her because she tried so hard to look nice for the visit. It's people like that for whom I wanted to do everything I could to help their pet. Another visit was kind of scary. The client was a tall, large man who was neatly dressed, with combed back black hair full of product. While watching me lubricate a thermometer, lift his cat's tail up, and insert it, he asked if I ever took my own rectal temperature. I went pale. He was between me and the door; I felt trapped. He was staring down at me waiting for an answer. I had none to give. Then he continued, "I wonder what that would be like?" That did it! I murmured something to him about meeting him out at the front desk as I slithered past him, back plastered to the wall, with my arm hyper extended towards the doorknob.

The Ivory Tower of academia followed me to my first job. In those days, each state had their own licensing requirements. Some states had interviews, like Maine. For the Maine licensing exam, I went to a basement in a small town church that had six doors down a narrow hallway. Behind each door was a veterinarian from the state board. One interviewer was an equine vet who asked me to interpret x-rays of a hoof and name horse breeds. At the end he offered me a job. He must have been desperate. I didn't know half the breeds and did not have a clue what was on the x-ray. As I went through one door after another I felt like I was being interviewed by the Angel Gabriel at the Pearly Gates of Heaven. Nowadays I believe the Maine licensing exam consists of reviewing the state's unique animal laws and taking an open book test. Much more civilized.

Other states, like Connecticut, simply used the National Board scores. Connecticut did not accept my score of 242 as qualifying. I cannot tell you to this day what 242 means, but whatever it meant, it wasn't high enough. So I was given a provisional license until I retook the exam. As long as I worked with a licensed vet I was legal. The National Boards always scared me. I never was a good test taker. The test covered everything, and I mean everything: clinical procedures, pharmaceutics, parasitology, diseases, immunology, and nutrition. Anatomy for all domestic species and wildlife medicine was thrown in for good measure. What was I going to do? Take out years of school notes and my textbooks? That was crazy talk! I decided to read the *Merck Manual* from cover to cover, all 1676 pages. The *Merck Manual* is the encyclopedia of veterinary medicine. I believe human medicine has one too. Every night after a day of trying to be a vet, I sat down and read as much as I could before I nodded off to unconsciousness. It is very technical reading, nothing like an exciting John Grisham page-turner. I prayed my subconscious retained what I was reading. Three months later I sat down with the 50 other veterinarians the state deemed unqualified and retook the Boards. I got my score in two weeks, and I passed—Connecticut granted me my license. My score was ... 242. Exactly the same as my first score! I was relieved yet cynical about the process. I was done with tests and the arbitrary hoops states put vets through.

My first job was hard work, long hours, challenging, rewarding, heartbreaking, and an education in itself. I never stopped learning. I was a student of my profession until the day I retired 32 years later—pretending to be a vet all the while.

\* \* \* \*

Afterthoughts by Dr Jefferson:

The new guy vs old guy in practice is something we all go through until we are battle tested. Luckily I started to gray on top quite early and that helped my acceptance a little. John's boss taking off after John had just been there three months was actually a wise thing to do. He had assessed John and knew that when he came back after ten days, the place would still be standing, and he'd find John more assured. I'm betting that every one of John's client interactions in those ten days left them all happy with him and more than willing to have him take care of their animals. John's story of the lab tests he ran on the lipoma dog is common to all of us when we start out in practice. With time and seasoning we don't order quite as much lab work. We slowly develop an accurate gut instinct as to what is going on with a patient. That's why they call it practice.

## Dr Jefferson: My First Job

My first job out of vet school was with Dr Fred Erb of Landaff, New Hampshire. Fred had an old fashioned set of values and the respect of all his clients. He was proud of his German heritage. He was not a particularly tall man, but he had a barrel chest, a deep voice, and was very strong. He also had a loud "Har de har har" laugh you could hear the next farm over. The episode that characterizes Fred for me happened during my first year of working for him. I had called for help. He gave me that, but also gave me a good standing with a client when he could have thrown me under the bus.

I was on a dystocia case in a cow named Blossom. The word dystocia means difficult birth, and that is what she was going through. Blossom was a black and white Holstein, which is one of the bigger breeds. Fortunately, the farm was just a ten minute drive from the office. Harry, her owner, told me that Blossom had been straining for a few hours with no results. He stood next to her hind end and held her tail around to the side so it wouldn't be in my way. I first put on a plastic glove and sleeve and lubricated it to do a rectal exam for a quick evaluation. In cows the rectal exam gives lots of information. As you feel through the rectal wall, you are able to explore the uterus, ovaries, and the fetus. I didn't have to go in much past my forearm to feel the fetus's head and forelegs. He or she was in the right position, head and forelegs heading toward the birth canal. I started bouncing the calf by pushing down over its shoulders. The calf reacted by pulling away. That was good news. We had a live calf.

I backed out of the rectum and pulled off the sleeve that was coated with Blossom's manure. Then I washed her hind end with soap and water until everything was squeaky clean. After that I rolled up the sleeve of my shirt and scrubbed my right arm and hand. I pulled on a sterile glove and sleeve and applied lubricant liberally up and down my arm. Then I coned my hand and gently slid it into Blossom's birth canal.

I was able to grab one of the calf's feet, but that's all. I kept wondering, she seems to want to calve, and all of her pelvic ligaments are relaxed, but why is there no room in here. Everything felt very cramped. What was I missing? After a couple of minutes I realized I was over my head. I pulled the sleeve off and said to Harry, "I really don't know what's going on here. I'm going to see if Dr Erb is at home."

I called Fred on the vehicle Motorola radio (this was long before cell phones) and was relieved to get him right away. "Fred, I'm over my head on a calving case at Harry's. Can you come bail me out?"

As we waited for Fred's arrival I made small talk with Harry. As we talked I felt restless, wondering what I was missing with this birth. Fred arrived, joking with everyone as he always did. After scrubbing up, he lubed up his arms and dove in. No sterile sleeves for Fred. He always said, "I can feel more this way." He fussed around for about five minutes, did some grunting, used a lot of body mechanics, got up a mild sweat, and then said, "There, I think I got things going. I'm pooped. You take back over." I did, and now everything inside that cow made sense. There was the calf's head, cradled as it should be on its front legs. What did Fred do in there? I delivered a rambunctious bull calf.

Back at the office he sat me down. "That was a uterine torsion. It was about as complete a twist as I've ever seen. When the uterus is twisted like that, it rotates the whole birth canal. It's no wonder you couldn't make heads or tails of it."

"We learned about it in school, but I've never seen one, and I'm not sure I have the strength to correct it like you did."

"That didn't take strength. All that grunting was a show put on for Harry so he wouldn't think you were a dumb-dumb."

"Well, it looked like you were working hard."

"Nope. I had the correction done right away. What you do is slide your hand into the birth canal and follow the folds to find out how complete the torsion is and in what direction it is going: clockwise or counterclockwise. Then you grab one of the calf's legs and push straight ahead. For just a second the calf is floating in the uterine fluid. Use the leg you have as a lever to flip the calf's body over. The uterus will unwind at the same time. It just takes some coordination."

It was one more thing I wasn't taught in vet school. I said that Dr Erb was very strong. I tried flipping these cases after that, but just didn't have the upper body strength to flip things around.

Some vets will roll a cow with a uterine twist onto her back and lay a plank across her abdomen. Believe it or not, one or two men stand on the plank, and two more roll the cow in the correct direction. The pressure of the plank makes the uterus stay in one spot, and the cow untwists around it. If this sounds complicated, it is; and truth be told, I was never able to make it work myself.

In any event, Harry never knew how Fred saved face for me that day, and I was always grateful for that kindness.

Fred's practice did have a modest small animal hospital, and occasionally I would get trapped into seeing a dog or a cat on an emergency basis if the boss was out of town. He soon learned not to make routine small animal appointments for me as I know I lost some clients for him. I always felt awkward trying to squeeze into the role of small animal vet. I'm sure most of the clients picked up on my discomfort and, of course, the animals always did. One day a client brought in a dog with a problem. I had only been out of school a few months. After my exam I announced what the diagnosis was. The owner looked me in the eye and said, "I don't believe you. I think you're wrong."

I immediately turned very red, and without thinking (obviously), replied, "You know, I don't believe me either." He grabbed his dog and left. As he left, I said softly, "By the way, you don't owe me anything for the visit."

Over the shoulder came his reply, "You got that right." We never saw him again. After that Fred pretty much kept me on the road where I usually didn't lose clients. From day one I was at home in any barn or stable, where I was more apt to be relaxed. The owners knew it, and the cows knew it.

After a couple of years working for Fred little things were beginning to niggle at me. I thought I was ready to have my own practice and began looking at large animal practices for sale. This was 50 plus years ago, long before the internet, so my search was limited to checking ads at the back of veterinary journals. The one that sounded most interesting was a large animal practice in rural western Pennsylvania. That meant getting that state's veterinary license. Today there is a federal exam recognized by all states. Back then each state was quite territorial, and you had to pass each state's exam if you wanted to practice there. I wrote the Veterinary Board of Pennsylvania and got an invitation to come and take their exam and interview. When I left vet school, I thought exams and interviews were a thing of the past. It was hard starting the process all over again.

The drive from New Hampshire to Logan airport in Boston took four hours. Then it was a nonstop flight to Philadelphia to take the exam. There was no studying as there was no predicting what would be on the exam. Aardvarks to Zebras and everything in between. It was all fair game.

I picked up my very first rental car ever at the Philadelphia airport. In hindsight I should have taken a cab. Driving through downtown Philly without the benefit of a GPS was exciting. Lost isn't the word for it. No one I asked was even aware that there was a vet school in town. At one point I ended up in South Philly and got a taste of what it's like to be a foreigner. Mine was the only white face to be seen for blocks. I crisscrossed the city many times until finally, by sheer luck, stumbled on a brass sign on a brick wall that said Pennsylvania Veterinary College. The receptionist at the school took me to a large classroom where some 30 other candidates were waiting. We sat in rows, looking at the back of the person in front of us. Our instructions were to listen for our name and leave with the examiner. After an hour I heard, "Jefferson, David Jefferson." I jumped up and followed the voice. In the hallway Dr Amos Benson introduced himself. He looked to be about 60. He had a pot belly, gray hair and reading spectacles balanced on the tip of his nose. We walked together down a long hallway. Why did this feel like the last mile? Finally he turned into an interview room where a bulging briefcase was setting on a chair. He offered me a seat, removed the briefcase from his, and we both sat down. Dr Benson explained that the state of Pennsylvania gave its examiners total latitude in testing candidates. His preference was oral exams. He told me he was a small animal practitioner with a special interest in radiography and had brought along a bunch of radiographs. He reached into his bulging brief case and pulled out a large x-ray film envelope.

I stuffed back the panic I was feeling. In the past two years in a dairy cattle practice there had been no exposure to dog x-rays. I had examined only a few dogs and certainly hadn't seen many radiographs since graduation.

"Now," Dr Benson began, "these are films of a four-year-old male Cocker Spaniel. He started vomiting after breakfast and has been retching since. He was brought to you in the late afternoon, same day. His vital signs and blood work are on this sheet of paper. X rays were taken of his abdomen. Here they are. " Dr Benson slipped the x-rays into a viewer on the desk and flicked on the light. "I will give you some time to review the clinical notes and look at the films. You are to give me a primary diagnosis, a differential diagnosis, a treatment plan and a prognosis for this dog. You have ten minutes to review the information, come up with your answer and then be prepared to answer my questions. Your time starts now."

Thoughts rocketed through my mind. I thought about me getting up at 3 a.m. that day to fly out of Boston in time for an exam somewhere in Philly at 4 p.m.. I thought about me in panic mode trying to find this building. I thought that this whole experience was going to end very poorly. There was no way I could bluff through it. Anything I might luckily notice in the exam report or on the x-rays would just lead to pointed questions and an even deeper hole for me. Dr Benson would realize within minutes that he had a complete nincompoop on his hands, a *wannabe* Pennsylvania vet who was pretty cheeky in even applying to take this examination. I paused for a moment, took a deep breath and said, "Dr Benson, could we just chat for a moment first."

Dr Benson tipped back in his chair, looked at me over his reading specs, paused a long minute, and then said, "Well ... yes, of course."

"Sir, my dream all through vet school was to become a large animal vet. I did the four years at Cornell which, of course, included the small animal courses. I graduated, but for sure have forgotten 95% of the small animal stuff, which until this minute, has never bothered me. I have been working in rural New Hampshire and have examined maybe six dogs since vet school. You will be able to make mincemeat out of me if I make any attempt to tell you what ails your Cocker Spaniel." I felt like adding: "I throw myself on the mercy of the court."

Dr Benson took off his glasses and rubbed his eyes. He stared at me for a long minute. I decided to meet his gaze. Then he asked, "Are

*Dog and Pony Show*

you a coffee drinker?"

"Yes, sir, I am."

"Come with me." I followed Dr Benson out of the building and around the corner into a coffee shop.

Over the coffee Dr Benson and I talked about our families. We talked about our mutual love of animals. We shared the kind of war stories that vets always tell each other. In half an hour Dr Benson, who now insisted on being called Amos, said, "David, I get it. Years ago I forgot everything I ever learned about horses or cattle in vet school, and wouldn't want to be tested on my knowledge, ever. I appreciate your honesty and believe that if you came to this state you would be a credit to the profession. Besides that, I like you as a person. Let me ask you a question. If you do come to practice in Pennsylvania, will you promise me that you will never examine or treat a dog or a cat?"

I raised my right hand. "I do so solemnly swear."

"Congratulations! You have just passed the State of Pennsylvania veterinary boards. Look for your license in the mail." Amos shook my hand and wouldn't even let me pay for the coffee. I never did end up in Pennsylvania. A few years later I got tired of paying the annual license fee and let my Pennsylvania license expire. I stayed in New England with no regrets. In the years since, I have never forgotten my crazy trip to Philadelphia and my friend, the remarkably understanding, Dr Amos Benson.

\* \* \* \*

Afterthoughts by Dr Hunt:

Dave's experience as a new vet takes a page right out of James Harriot's *All Creatures, Great and Small* books. That kind of stuff really does happen. What a wonderful story. You can feel Dave's angst while his brain was frantically trying to figure things out—because that is what vets do: figure things out. No two animals present the same disease in the same way, nor do they respond to treatment in the same way.

I found it interesting that Dr Benson paid for David's coffee. Because every time David and I had coffee together he somehow wiggled out of paying for it! You got to watch out for personable guys like David. They have a way at getting free coffee.

# Chapter 5

## Influencers

# Dr Hunt: My Pinball Life

My life is like the silver ball in a pinball machine. The plunger shoots me out into the playing field, and as I work my way down to the exit hole, my ball engages in bumpers, holes, obstacles, and targets, all changing my direction and speed. If the ball gets near the exit hole, the flippers in front shoot it back into the playing field for another series of bumps and obstacles. When the silver ball comes in contact with a bumper, it careens off it, changing its direction in unpredictable ways, influencing how the game proceeds.

People we meet and know can act as the bumpers that influence the silver ball of our lives by teaching us life's lessons, guiding our moral compasses, or setting examples to emulate or avoid. Influences can lead you away from bad choices as much as direct you to good ones.

My parents influenced me by example. My dad was a professor of psychology, my mom a special education teacher. Education was the fabric of my life. I ended up getting three degrees and becoming a teacher, a coach, and a writer—all of which I integrated into my career and raising my three children. My dad's sense of humor you can see in all of my chapters in this book. My writing style came from my mom. I have a large folder of her missives about raising four children with her psychologist husband—a P*lease Don't Eat the Daisies* kind of collection.

My track coaches were also significant influences during my teenage years. My senior year cross country coach was actually a football coach who was asked to take over the cross country team. He knew nothing about running, but he sought advice, listened to our ideas, and, most importantly, respected the team. He taught me to seek help when I needed it and to respect the people who tried to help me. We ended up going undefeated that year and became league champs. My track coach was also a big influence on how to manage, motivate, and get results from people, but he did it in a subtle, understated way. He taught me that less is better. His coaching style depended on the trust and respect his athletes had for him and the sport. With that he was able to coach 35 high school kids in 16 different events, by himself! He seemed confident on how to coach an event, and he trusted us to do a workout even if he was not supervising. We weren't angels, though—we were teenage boys. We mooned people from the back of the bus, got caught going to parties with alcohol, and even sent an underclassmen out to the athletic field dressed only in a paper bag. But Coach would reel us back in with a, "Damn it, Hunt, knock it off." He was loved by all because we saw that he truly loved us. His coaching taught me that working hard gets results and being sincere goes a long way when managing people.

I spent a year in East Lansing prior to getting into vet school, and there I worked under vets who would help form the type of teacher and vet I would become. I worked at a busy, well-known, highly respected mixed animal practice as the "back room" tech. I prepped animals for surgery, medicated and monitored sick patients, and did all of the heartworm tests in the lab—all 2000 of them. One day, one of the owners, an elderly, white haired, amiable man with a most disarming smile, walked in from the exam rooms with a dog that needed to be put to sleep. He called me over and told me that I needed to give the IV injection in the leg. I was a nervous wreck. My boss was restraining the little poodle and I had to get the needle in the vein. I was shaking like a leaf and kept missing. My boss didn't move, he kept holding the dog and kept encouraging me in a soft, calm voice. I finally got the vein and got a "good job" and smile out of my boss. I never forgot his patience and calm. I tried to emulate that any time I was training a technician, client, or student. In the same practice I went out with the large animal vet on a farm call. We had to castrate about 20 piglets. We found them in a small barn enclosed in a makeshift paddock. Dr S casually said, "John, go in get a piglet. All you need to do is grab a rear leg to catch one."

I must have looked cocky, like this was going to be easy. I thought, *I can show Dr S how helpful I can be on farm calls.* I eagerly jumped in the paddock, and much to my surprise, the rodeo began. I was running around after those piglets like a circus clown for five minutes before I caught one. Dr S was smiling the whole time. I learned to be humble and not take myself too seriously that day.

That same year, I learned that some influencers would teach me what not to do. On weekends I had a second job as a kennel person for a vet who owned about five small animal hospitals in the Lansing area. He was more of an entrepreneur than a vet. One Saturday morning, as I was shoveling poop, I watched the vet give a cat a bath. The cat was becoming out of control, trying to bite and scratch the vet. Instead of stopping, the vet slammed the cat down on the tub and almost drowned the poor thing. I was appalled. I learned there is a difference between being stern and being abusive. I vowed never to cross that line.

Consequently, I actually molded the way I wanted to run a veterinary practice more from what I didn't want to do. For instance, one of my bosses in Connecticut used to leave sticky notes at the back entrance where the employees entered the building saying, "John, see me." I found that rude, passive aggressive, and just plain unprofessional. Put yourself in my place—I'm walking into the clinic first thing in the morning, wondering if I'm going to be scolded for something.

I worked at three different vet hospitals before going out on my own. My bosses influenced how I practiced medicine. I eavesdropped on the senior practice owner of a five-man hospital I worked at who was counseling a client having to make a decision to put her dog to sleep. He was empathetic, yet straightforward. He seemed to know that his client was in a real emotional bind. He was able to help the owner make her own decision and provide emotional support at the same time. And he did it more by listening than talking. Now that takes finesse. My first boss, of German stock, let me get myself out of my own jams (see my "Oops" chapter) yet had my back if a client was being difficult—a philosophy I embraced in my practice with my associates.

I've had plenty of times where the flippers kept me from going down the exit hole. When tragedy came my way, I needed to be strong yet seek help to get me through. Divorce, losing a baby, being sued, getting robbed, the death of a parent, and personal illness all knocked me off course. But family and friends, as well as the strength I drew from what I learned from my influencers, flipped me back into life.

We all have influencers that directly or indirectly mold us into what we are today. It is an ongoing process. As we move around the playing field, we hit new bumpers that change our direction, and get flipped back into the game if we happen to be down and out. The Pinball Wizard is always there to give you a fortuitous jolt without tilting.

Dr John H. Hunt and Dr David A. Jefferson

\* \* \* \*

Afterthoughts by Dr Jefferson:

I love the analogy of John feeling like the silver ball in a pinball machine! Parents, coaches, and bosses all have the potential of bouncing us off in unplanned directions, often not gently. The picture of young John trying to impress Dr S with his ability to catch piglets was fun to read. Lots easier said than done. Yes, and humbling for sure. John, next time we're together and near a litter of little pigs, I'll give you a lesson on how to catch 'em. Wear your old clothes and a sense of humor. I promise not to video it. (sort of)

John had a successful practice because he used both the good *and* the poor examples he had experienced to build his own personality and career. The animals he treated and the clients that brought them in, all reaped the benefits of him having been careened here and there in life.

# Dr Jefferson: My Mentors

*Grandma Topsy*: My mom's mom. She lived with us. I remember her smell and how her lap was just right for sitting in as she read me stories. She taught me the alphabet and how to see early words in all those mysterious scribbles. Incredible! I've loved reading ever since. She was hard of hearing. I inherited that. Now I wear hearing aids. Mine have a tiny battery tucked into the curved unit that hooks over the ear and are almost unnoticeable. Hers were in a battery case the size of a cigarette pack, hidden somewhere in that mysterious area down her front. I think it's called a bodice. Two pink twisted wires ran up from there to her ears. Without her hearing aids she was pretty deaf, unless one of us was whispering something they didn't want her to hear.

*Bess Solloway:* My 4th grade teacher. The writing assignment was, "What I Am Good At." I was never great at sports, which were what the rest of the class seemed to be writing about. I couldn't think of anything, so I wrote about how I helped Mom around the house. I wrote that I would carry the clunky Hoover vacuum cleaner up and down the stairs for her. Miss Solloway read my paper aloud. I was unbelievably embarrassed. I wanted the floor to open up so I could sneak out through a basement window. I think she sensed that. Later in the day she pulled me aside and told me she was proud of me. Never forgot it. I love her to this day. Maybe she kindled my love of writing.

*Sheldon Merritt*: My goal as a teenager was to own my own dairy farm. As mentioned in Chapter 1, the college I attended after high school was Delhi Tech, a two-year community college in upstate New York. Professor Merritt taught animal husbandry. I was just 17, and I'm guessing he was in his late 60s. One day he said, "People talk about the success of others and they call it luck. I think you make a good deal of your own luck." I never forgot that.

After my retirement I taught vet tech students at a community college. I was what they call an adjunct professor. That means they trusted me to teach the courses, but they weren't sure I could handle the money, so they didn't pay well. That's OK. I think I took the job as payback. Community college was a perfect start for me. I am able to say to my freshman classes today, "If you want, you can go on from here." I tell them I did. I hope some remember it and don't get satisfied too early in life.

*John McHale, Sergeant, United States Marine Corps:* My drill instructor at recruit training, Parris Island, South Carolina, July 1960, Platoon 364. A man about as tough as they come. Saw action in the Pacific in WWII. He was part of the invasion force on the island of Tarawa, where 12,000 Marines landed. In three days 1000 Marines died, and over 2000 were wounded on that 1/2 square mile island. 800 were buried right on the beach—three days of hell—but it opened the way for the rest of the Japanese-held islands. McHale was a Marine's Marine. When I don't feel brave enough to tackle something, I think of McHale. He probably didn't want to leave the landing craft when its ramp dropped on the beach— He did it anyway.

*Math Teacher, Cornell*: Can't remember her name, but she saved my college career. I was right out of the Marine Corps and hadn't cracked a text book in three years. I had been accepted at Cornell as an undergrad and needed to finish my studies to apply to the vet school. I had never done well in math, and my scores on the SATs for math from high school were dismal. The Cornell administration wisely sent me to what was like a junior high resource room. It was really "math for dummies." This wonderful lady knew how embarrassed and frustrated I was at my lack of math skills. She worked patiently with me that whole first semester. Under her guidance, I began to understand and appreciate math for the first time in my life.

*Dr Francis Fox, Vet School professor, Large Animal Medicine*: In our junior year he gave an entire course on the science and art of physical diagnosis. It's been more than 50 years, and I can still hear him saying:

"Use all your senses: look, look again, listen, feel, get your nose right down there and smell! If you have to, taste it!" I was in his office one day in my senior year, and he asked me to go out to the cow barn and examine the calf in the first stall.

"Come back and tell me what you find."

20 minutes later I reported back: "She's got a pronounced systolic heart murmur audible on both sides. It sounds like a valvular insufficiency." Oh yeah, I was pretty proud of myself.

"What else?"

"That's all I found."

"Go back and look again."

I used my stethoscope, my ophthalmoscope, my ears, my eyes, and yes, my nose. I finally found something else and reported back.

"Her tail has a kink in it, half way up. I think she must have fractured it."

"Nope, she was born with it. It's called wry tail, spelled w-r-y. It's often seen in calves with congenital heart issues. So if you run into another calf with wry tail, check the heart. If it's got that murmur, onto the veal truck with her as she won't live long. It's rare to find one congenital problem without another. They go in pairs, sometimes in triplets. Next time don't stop your exam until you have looked at everything. Got that?"

"Yes, sir."

"Don't forget it."

Never did. And, from that day on, right through the day I left vet school, he called me "wry tail."

*Writers Group at Gulfport, Florida Senior Center*: You have listened to my stories, encouraged me, challenged me, and have kept me writing. I look on each and every one of you as a good friend. From the bottom of my heart, thank you.

*My clients*: What a great bunch of people. I loved the fact that they consistently put the needs of their animals first, often sacrificing for them. They were forgiving of my mistakes and almost all became good friends.

*My wife, Bonnie*: We've been married 56 years. She put me through vet school, and then I was so busy running the practice that she mostly raised our two kids. All the credit that they turned out well is due to her. In my close to 50 years running my own business I never once heard a complaint about my long hours or me showing up late for supper again, smelling like a horse. Now, she is making retirement a new fun adventure.

Dr John H. Hunt and Dr David A. Jefferson

* * * *

Afterthoughts by Dr Hunt:

Getting to know Dave through the people that influenced him gave me new insight as to who my newfound friend and co-author is. Thanks for sharing. Your pinball game had a lot of bumpers that rewarded you with free games.

# Chapter 6
# A Dangerous Profession

# Dr Hunt: Staying Safe

A very common question I get from people is, "Have you ever been bitten?" Maybe they ask that just to start a conversation. Secretly I'm thinking, *Well, duh—what do you think?* A subtle version of that question that challenges my expertise as a vet is, "How many times have you been bitten?" If I say never, they know I'm lying, but any number I give will be an admission of my shortcomings as a vet. Veterinarians are supposed to love all animals at all times and, conversely, all animals are supposed to love all veterinarians. I call this the Dr Doolittle Syndrome. When a terrified dog in pain came into my exam room and tried to bite me and I heard the owner exclaim, "He has never done that before!" it felt like the subliminal message was that I was a failure as a vet.

All of that to say—yes, I've been bitten! I've also been scratched, attacked, peed on, pooped on, bled on, slobbered on, vomited on, sneezed on, squirted on by anal glands, spewed on from a ruptured abscess, spit at (by a cat), almost knocked over, and even pushed by a client. Not the most glamorous part of my profession. I took it all in stride. It was in the job description, but in the very small fine print at the bottom of the page.

In 32 years as a veterinarian, I am proud to say I've actually been bitten by a dog only a handful of times. With cats it was usually a one two punch of a bite on the hand and scratches up the arm. I've had one too many nips from hamsters, birds, and even a monkey bite when I was a town recreation counselor in high school.

Most bites happened when I got distracted and failed to pay attention, or the situation forced me into a dangerous position. One time when my son, who was about four years old at the time, was quietly sitting at my desk coloring, an excited, aggressive dog broke from a leash held by my technician. The dog was charging towards the office where my son was sitting. I leaped between the dog and my son, reached out to grab the collar, and was bitten on the hand for my efforts.

Believe it or not, it was the little lap dogs that posed the greatest danger. Trying to pry them from the clutches of their nervous owner for examination was always a challenge, especially when the owner was a large woman who nestled the dog between her breasts. I was not only in danger of getting bitten, but also getting slapped for being fresh. When the little lap dog was standing alone on the exam table, their fear meter went off the scale. Away from Mom, on a steel table, the smells of a vet clinic, and a strange man coming at them with large hands holding something that was definitely not a treat or toy—a perfect storm.

With large dogs I could read their body language as they entered the room. Many times I would be seated in the exam room as my client and patient entered. As I greeted my client I would observe the dog. I let it explore the room and it would eventually come to me for a sniff and greeting. A dog that was super nervous would stand behind the owner, cowering, with its tail tucked between its legs and its ears plastered to the head. A dog with a hostile attitude faced me while standing behind their owner, ears up and forward, and tail up. Once they were on the exam table I always watched for the look, which is when a dog shows you the whites of their eyes. I don't know how they do it, and it is hard to explain. Sometimes all seemed okay until, while I was auscultating the heart, I felt the dog stiffen and I heard thunder—the dog growling in my stethoscope. Once the dog gave any warning signal, and most did, I brought out the muzzle. As a young vet I hesitated to muzzle because I felt obligated to be Dr Doolittle. At some point in my career, I realized I needed to perform my job to help my patients, and muzzling was a way to successfully accomplish my task. Some owners frowned on muzzles because they thought it was cruel. My soft nylon muzzle fit like a sock so it didn't look menacing, and I got to the point where I simply explained that it had to be done for me to help their pet, that it didn't hurt, and would actually calm the dog down.

I only had one or two clients in my career that wouldn't let me muzzle. One situation in particular became a circus every time the client brought his 100 pound German Shepherd in for a nail trim. The client, Roger, and his wife, Pru, were some of my favorite clients. Pru usually brought in their cats, of which they had many. She was a beautiful woman with 1950s style hair, all fluffed out, but she made it work. Office visits with Roger were a mixture of a social visit and outright hell. The first thing he did when he came into the exam room was tell me a few jokes.

Some were good, some corny, and some stupid, but they were always funny to me. Then the work began. He couldn't cut his dog's nails at home and he didn't like muzzles. He used to say "Doc," (he always called me Doc for some reason) "let's get Bruiser on the table and I'll hold him." I know why he couldn't cut Bruiser's nails at home. The dog went absolutely crazy when the nail clippers came out of the cabinet. And I mean crazy! It took forever because with each nail I trimmed, Bruiser tried to reach back and bite me while Roger did everything he could to keep his head forward. On top of that, Bruiser would try to yank his paw away when I got close to a nail, just like a horse or cow. I swear my fingers were in danger of amputation with every nail. But we always got it done. Once off the exam table, Bruiser turned into his friendly, well-disciplined self. As Roger and I were wiping sweat off our brows, he would tell one last joke, we would chuckle between sighs of relief, and off they would go until the next time.

I had an elderly client that had a Chow Chow that, how can I put this, simply didn't like me. I couldn't do anything with him. He growled when I even looked at him. I offered to dispense tranquilizers before the visit or to put him under general anesthesia like I did with other hard to handle pets (except Bruiser, of course), but she would have none of that. Finally, I told her that her dog and I didn't see eye to eye and maybe she should try another vet. This was the first time I fired a client. She mumbled something I couldn't understand. I assumed she agreed with me. The next month she came in for a visit. I entered the exam to see the Chow scowling, ready to do battle, and the woman just as calm as can be sitting in the chair. I exclaimed, "I thought you were going to another vet?" She responded, "I like you, Dr Hunt. I want you to be my vet," and so the battle continued.

Cats were a very different story. They had teeth and four claws with sharp nails—and they used them all at once. A scared cat that gets loose in a room is a nightmare. I have had cats literally climb up a door, tear down window shades, clear off a countertop full of medical equipment, and run horizontally on a wall three feet off the floor like a Bugs Bunny cartoon. Their bites are deep and their scratches are painful. A cat can change its mood on a dime. During an exam I was always looking at the cat's ears. Up and forward was fine, down and back—stop what you're doing. Cats can explode into the Tasmanian Devil in a millisecond. Muzzling sometimes helped, but wrapping the cat in a towel was the most popular restraint technique I used. I had two backup restraints standing by for explosions. One was a canvas bag snapped onto aluminum handles. The handles allowed me to open and close the bag. I could corner the sweet pussy cat-turned-devil and capture it safely. It also had zippered openings so I could get access to the cat. It was affectionately called "the cat bag." I also had the "cat cage," which was a small squeeze cage that safely restrained unruly cats. Getting scared cats out of a cat carrier in the exam room was a challenge. None of my restraint tools could help. Reaching in a small cat carrier with only one hand while the cat was plastered against the back was suicidal. Even Dr. Doolittle would have trouble. I used to lift the carrier up on end and shake it till the cat gave up and poured out the door onto the table. At that point, most cats were resigned to their fate and sat quietly, but not happily, on a towel.

Small exotics like rabbits, rats, mice, and guinea pigs were usually okay. For birds, proper restraint in a towel and a wooden dowel in the mouth prevented potentially serious bites. The hamster was another story. When a hamster came in I was resigned to being bitten. My fate was sealed. Hamsters that are handled a lot at home are wonderful little pets, but most of the hamsters I saw were semi-wild because no one petted or handled them. The hamster cages were small and included an exercise wheel, cardboard tubes, and toys, so the little angel could run and hide. And they are small with no tails! Try grabbing a scared, furry little creature that can scurry into a tube or behind an exercise wheel by the scruff of what you think is a neck. Don't—you will get bitten! Trapping them in a tube was my best strategy.

I can't talk about animal restraint without mentioning Bobbie the cat. His owner was a middle aged man who had a very soft, quiet voice that matched his demeanor. He was the kind of guy who would walk past you on the street and you wouldn't be able to recall him. I could see his love for Bobbie in his eyes every time he brought Bobbie into the clinic. Bobbie was a 14-pound tabby that projected an air of confidence, and even a hint of royalty, in the way he sat and looked at you. The unusual thing about Bobbie was that the owner always carried him into the exam room in a cardboard box bottom with an old towel lining. Bobbie wouldn't move a muscle. He sat tall and quiet, seemingly oblivious to all the goings on at the clinic. He didn't look scared or friendly, but regal, unconcerned, and completely in control of the situation. When I first met Bobbie the owner murmured that it would be best to keep Bobbie in the cardboard box during the visit. I respected the request. The visits were smooth. Bobbie let me look him over and give him shots. He never moved a muscle. He accepted me because he knew his owner trusted me. He was a special cat. One day, Bobbie was brought in because he wasn't feeling well. His eyes looked tired and he was a little hunched in his box. He tried to maintain his usual aloof acceptance of being at the clinic, but couldn't quite pull it off. After I examined Bobbie I felt I needed some blood work to get a better idea of what might be wrong with him, so I recommended I keep Bobbie for a few hours so I could draw blood. For the first time I saw the owner's mild mannered, quiet face turn scared. He wasn't sure if he wanted to leave Bobbie. The owner had known me for years. I knew his parents and all his brothers and sisters in town. His fears gave way to his trust in me. So I picked up the box and carried Bobbie to the hospital kennels in the back. He never moved a muscle even after I shut the kennel door. After seeing a few office calls I had a few minutes free so I decided to draw Bobbie's blood. I opened the kennel door, talking to Bobbie all the while, and started to pick him up out of his box. Instantly Bobbie turned into one of the most aggressive cats I had encountered. He flew into a rage—snarling, growling, spitting, biting, and scratching. I barely got the door closed before being torn to shreds. I left the hospital ward with my heart racing and beads of sweat on my forehead. I couldn't believe it. All these years he never gave me an ounce of trouble. *It must be the box*, I thought, *he's okay if he is in the box.* I returned to the kennel after I recovered from the scare, and there was Bobbie sitting calmly in the box. I opened the door—so far so good—I picked up the box—all is well—and placed it on the hospital treatment table. With Bobbie still in his box, my technician lifted his head so I could draw blood from his jugular vein in the neck. Bobbie never moved a muscle. Bobbie's owner returned a nervous wreck. He was upset about leaving Bobbie and of course nervous about the results of the blood work. I assured the owner

Bobbie behaved admirably during the blood draw and all he had was an infection that could be treated. I never took Bobbie out of his box after that day.

I need to vent here, so bear with me. It was really irritating to hear from a client, after their dog just bit me, that, "Gee, she never did that before." I kept my composure and refrained from making a smart ass response like, "Yeah, right!" because I was busy washing the wound and wrapping it with a sterile gauze. Dogs and cats are really very civilized. When they get mad or scared, they give off all sorts of signals with their body and voice. Reading an animal's body language will give you all you need to know about what the pet is feeling. Prior to a dog ever biting a person for the first time, they advertise the upcoming bite by warning the target in hopes of not having to resort to a bite. If the warnings like growling, a stiff stance, ears forward or down and back, or hair raised on the back go unheeded, biting is the last resort. The dog feels that biting is the last and only message that will be listened to. So if a dog bit me in the exam room, I doubted that was the first time, or, if it was, then he had been giving warning signs in stressful situations at home for a while and standing on a slippery table in a vet clinic with a strange man holding a needle was the straw that broke the camel's back. One scenario that may explain a fearful dog biting for the first time during an office visit is because it can't escape like it can at home. Biting out of the blue with no warnings is rare, except in a case of rabies. The problem I encounter is by the time a dog gets to the clinic, it no longer feels the warnings work, so it skips most of them and goes right to the bite. Thank you for listening.

In all the decades I practiced medicine not one client threatened me with bodily harm, until about two months before I retired. A young man brought in his rather raucous, poorly controlled pit bull. The dog was dancing around the owner's legs, ears forward and hackles up—not a good sign. When it was time to get him on the exam table, I took the leash to guide the dog to the table. The dog flipped out, went up onto his rear legs, twirled around the leash, and fell. I still had the leash, so as he went to the floor the dog choked itself on the leash for about two seconds—the time it took for me to realize what was happening and released the leash. The kid stepped over to me and shoved me to the

*Dog and Pony Show*

wall. I was astounded and shocked. I told him to leave immediately. He apologized profusely and tried to justify his shove by saying I was hurting his dog. I explained what I was trying to do. He calmed down and we finished the office call. I wasn't planning on ever seeing him again, but he did continue to come in for vet work. What a way to end a career!

When your veterinarian recommends restraint for your pet, try to understand it is being done for everyone's safety. Your vet is there to perform a service, and some pets just won't have it. Fear and panic are the primary motivators to bite. It is no reflection on the pet, you, or the vet. It's just the way it is. Don't fight with your vet about bite prevention. Work with him so everyone is safe.

\* \* \* \*

Afterthoughts by Dr Jefferson:

I think John must have a magic way with dogs. To have only been bitten by a dog a handful of times! Remarkable! I don't work on dogs, but, like the mailman, I have been bitten many times. I was always leery on my first visit to any farm. Around from the side of the barn might come the farm dog at full speed with a mouthful of teeth. I agree with John, it's mostly the small ones. Is there such a thing as a small dog syndrome? They always went for my ankles, barking like angry seals. After getting nailed many times in my first year, when I got out of the truck, I always took the slim metal case that held my invoices. If a dog came too close, I offered that to bite on. A little tap on the top of the head for the persistent ones let them know I didn't appreciate the guard dog act. All vets, small or large animal, quickly learn to become good at reading animal body language. By the way, geese are the worse. They are sneaky and always come up from behind. They bite your ankles, and it hurts. Too bad that you missed the geese experience, John. I could give you a few addresses where geese are hanging around, anxious to see you.

# Dr Jefferson: It Goes With the Job

Unless their work is in a laboratory, any veterinarian you talk to will have his or her war stories of getting hurt by their patients. Large animal vets have their own unique encounters. In dealing with cattle and horses there is always the potential for serious injury. I have been the recipient of a few bites, countless kicks, many body slams, and lots of getting stepped on.

On more than one occasion I have been knocked flat on my back. Thirty years ago an Arabian horse recovering from general anesthesia got up too soon. He was completely disoriented, fell on me, and broke my leg. That followed my removal of his testicles, so we can count that injury as payback. It began a long, unplanned vacation.

A very opinionated race horse kicked me squarely in the crotch. Great aim! That ended that day's work. It was an uncomfortable ride home and the start of another vacation.

A friend of mine at vet school was too trusting with a dairy bull. The bull got him in a corner and pressed his head against him. That episode resulted in the removal of my friend's spleen and a few feet of intestine.

A body slam is when a horse wants to be in the space you are occupying and moves in fast. Done slowly and deliberately it's called crowding. When a horse weighing 1000 pounds moves into your space, you either give way or should have a plan to enable you to stand your ground. When you are in tight quarters with a horse, a plan going in is essential.

Years ago, when I first started in practice, most draft horses were housed in straight stalls, sometimes called slip stalls. These stalls have two high side walls and a front, but no rear wall. It's like a big wooden chute, six-feet wide and eight-feet long. The front is cut away so that you can access the manger, which is built into the front wall. Hay and grain can be delivered from the front of the stall so that you don't have to get in with the horse. Horses with feed anxiety don't pay much attention to the rules of proper behavior.

While straight stalls are rarely seen today, they are educational in teaching how to handle a horse in tight quarters. To lead a horse into a straight stall you walk in with him, on his left side, using a lead shank attached to his halter. At the front of the stall you pick up the end of a rope that is tied to an iron ring attached to the manger. There is a snap on the rope's free end that attaches to his halter. Once he is secured, you remove your lead and push against his left shoulder so that he will step over to give you some space to get out. The rope securing him is a few feet long. It's long enough so he can move around, but not so much that he can get a front leg over it. I am describing the stall in detail to highlight what a potentially dangerous place it can be if you are in there with a big horse.

Draft horses used to be the farm's power source, doing the hard work of plowing, planting, cultivating, logging, and haying. They usually weigh from 1500 to 2000 pounds. In the old days they were put up in straight stalls. Days, they were either worked or were in an outside pasture.

Straight stalls made for economical housing, as three horses can fit in the same space that one box stall would take up. The only time farmers would go into a straight stall themselves was when they were putting the horse in or taking him out. Grooming, harnessing, and shoeing were all done out on the barn floor. It was just too tight a space in the slip stall for you *and* the horse, especially if a horse had a tendency to crowd you or to panic.

When you are in a straight stall with a big horse and he moves in your direction, you can only back up so much and you'll encounter the wooden side wall behind you. Draft horses all had single syllable names for reasons of economy. Moms with kids with long names know that. Horses know their names and simple words like whoa. As they worked in teams, the preferred address is their name first and then the action you want them to take. "Bob, haw!" or "Sam, gee!" If you were in the horse's stall and he started to move your way, you would say, "Pete, git over!" and push against his shoulder. If that didn't work, your next move would be to slap him on the rib cage and repeat the command, but louder and sharper: "PETE! GIT OVER!" Occasionally that might be ignored too, and you are suddenly like the guy between a rock and a hard place. The horse may not respond because he is interested in getting to his feed and is not paying attention. Sometimes, rarely, you might have a willful horse on your hands.

An old-timer who worked his horses in the woods shared his knowledge with me about handling such situations. He always carried a 10-penny nail in his shirt pocket. A 10-penny is three inches long. If crowded by the horse, he would reach into this pocket, grab the nail and hold it in his fist with just about ½ inch of the point exposed. If the first, "Pete, git over," didn't get a response, he would hold the nail against the horse's side. It wasn't a jab, it was more like a steady push. Horses have very sensitive skin, and their immediate reaction is to quickly step away from anything sharp. It takes very little pressure and should always be accompanied by "Pete, git over!" so that the next time just the command will make the horse move. Another old timer told me, "No sir, I never use a nail. I make a fist with my left hand but leave my thumb sticking out. One good poke in the eye with my thumb and they move. Works every time." I can tell you from a couple of experiences, he was right.

Working with cattle and horses you have to be quick on your feet and be able to predict their next move. Horses, in particular, clearly telegraph what they are about to do. I call the expression on their face and their ear carriage the crystal ball. When you are around an animal that outweighs you, it's important to be aware of what their intentions are. If you are mindful, the chance of getting hurt is minimal. It's interesting that horses can be dangerous even as they are being euthanized. You can't predict which way a horse will fall in this procedure, and following your vet's exact instructions at that time is critical.

* * * *

Afterthoughts by Dr Hunt:

What I liked about Dave's chapter were the tricks he picked up from farmers, like the 10-penny nail story and how he used animal behavior to control the huge beasts he was obligated to treat.

As a small animal vet, if you ignored a pet's body language, and especially his eyes, you were dead meat. A nervous, painful, grouchy, sick dog or cat is not in the mood for some stranger to go poking around his body. Moving deliberately and modifying the exam or treatment depending on what the animal is telling you is essential.

I admire large animal vets for their courage and chutzpah in handling horses, bulls, and anything else larger than a Bull Mastiff..

# Chapter 7
## Prevention

# Dr Hunt: Kooties

Both small and large animal veterinarians are trained in the basics of epidemiology, which means vets are taught about the incidence, distribution, and control of diseases. One example we can all relate to as of 2021 is the control of the Coronavirus. Epidemiologists recommended wearing face masks, keeping a social distance from others, avoiding crowds (especially in an enclosed situation), and handwashing, especially before touching the face, to help control the spread of the virus.

Every day small animal veterinary hospitals have to be cognizant of disease control. Keeping the facility clean at all times reduces the opportunity for viruses and bacteria to establish themselves and become a danger to animals coming into the facility. During my 27 year tenure as owner of the Bucksport Veterinary Hospital, my staff's goal was to keep the facility clean so when clients came in they would not smell anything. I didn't want fragrances covering up odors. I wanted no odor at all. That served three purposes. One, people perceive a lack of odor as cleanliness. Two, some people are allergic to fragrances, so being odorless would eliminate reactions. Finally, any new, unwanted odors would be detected instantly. After each visit in the exam room, the tables would be cleaned and sterilized and the floor swept or mopped if necessary. Every night the entire clinic was wiped down and cleaned.

This reminds me of a funny little story. I took on a vet tech that had worked for a vet hospital in the next town. My staff and I knew her, so she fit right in. On her first day, to be helpful, she went to clean the exam table in the room I had just used. She sprayed the table with disinfectant and proceeded to unroll about ten sheets of paper towels to wipe down the table. I happened to witness this and nearly fainted. You have to understand that as an owner of a small business, keeping costs down was paramount. I ran into the room to ask what she was doing. She looked at me quizzically and answered, "Well, I'm cleaning the table for you." I thanked her but added, "You don't have to use half a roll of paper towels to do it."

She said, "I always did it that way at Dr A's clinic." I looked at the huge wad of paper towels as dollar bills. I didn't want to scold my new employee and friend on the first day, so I took a deep breath and said, "We just use one, maybe two sheets of paper towels to clean off the table," tried to grin, and walked into the reception area only to see the rest of my staff stifling a laugh. For years onward the Paper Towel Incident became a clinic joke. If any of us was seen using more than two sheets of paper towels, even when it was called for, the others would chastise them and laugh. It was a great joke used to introduce new employees.

Sometimes cleanliness needed to be kicked into high gear at a moment's notice. Sick animals with very contagious diseases needed to come to the clinic for medical help and were sometimes hospitalized. If a coughing dog or sneezing cat was scheduled to be looked at, our admission procedures changed. We needed to protect healthy pets visiting for other reasons from potentially contagious, airborne upper respiratory diseases, and face masks on a cat or a dog were not an option. My staff scheduled the potentially contagious pet when no other pets were in the waiting room. Upon arrival, the owner was to bring the pet directly into the exam room and go directly out after the office visit. The room was cleaned and the air was sprayed with antiviral solutions. I would change my lab coat.

For animals with contagious diseases that needed hospitalization, like the dreaded parvovirus diarrhea cases, we set the patient up in our isolation ward. Parvovirus is very infectious and very hardy outside the body, so extreme measures needed to be taken to prevent its spread within the hospital. We had a small room with a kennel at the end of a hallway as our isolation ward. Limited contact with staff and rigorous hand cleaning after treatment was required. In 1979 when the parvovirus first appeared and started killing dogs right and left, I was in vet school. We had to wear gowns, surgical caps, and gloves, and had to step in Clorox shoe baths before leaving the iso-ward.

And of course, surgeries had to be done under sterile conditions. Sterile instruments, sutures, drapes, gowns, and gloves were standard operating procedures. If you didn't follow the rules of sterility, your patients could get skin infections or internal infections.

I also had to be cognizant of zoonotic infections, which are infections that we could catch. Fighting diseases that were potentially harmful to humans was a delicate dance. You always had to be aware of personal dangers while treating the animal. One time while practicing in Connecticut I let my guard down. I was working at a very busy, four-man practice just outside Hartford, Connecticut. You can imagine how crazy it could get with four vets and numerous technicians attending to their patients under one roof all at the same time. As I was passing through the treatment area, I went by the x-ray machine where two techs were positioning a dog on its back for a radiograph. It had been hit by a car and had labored breathing. Just as I walked by, the dog stopped breathing. The technician yelled my name; I saw what was happening and immediately started to perform mouth to nose artificial respiration. As luck would have it the dog regained its breathing ability. I stopped and walked away. After about three steps it occurred to me that that dog could have had some zoonotic condition. I learned the dog died later that day. How stupid! What was I thinking? My mind raced to rabies. For weeks I was waiting to come down with rabies or bacterial pneumonia. That was 33 years ago and I still kick myself.

It was also my responsibility to make sure my clients were aware of the dangers their own sick pets may have posed to them. When a client brought in an itchy pet, I could see the person squirming in their clothes and keeping their pets at bay. Fleas were the number one cause of scratching, and fleas don't mind jumping on people for a meal. Most of the time the clients saw the flea and could at least kill it. Sarcoptic mange was another story. Even though the microscopic dog mange mite will not reproduce on people, they don't mind transferring onto you from the dog to spend a little time feeding on you. When a suspected mange dog came into the exam room, in order to help my diagnosis, I would coyly ask the owner if they were itchy. It got a little embarrassing at times because with women I needed to ask if they were itching under their bra strap. Mites love to stay under tight fitting clothes. I had to put on my most professional face and air of objectivity when asking. Remember, Bucksport is a very small town, and it wouldn't take much for a rumor warning women to steer clear of the vet to start. Rumors spread like a grass fire on the prairie. I could imagine the looks I would get at the grocery store if I stopped by for bread and milk at the end of the day. I found if I asked the bra question as part of a string of other places, very quickly, like, "Are you very itchy around your socks-bra-waist-arms," I avoided getting slapped and I could go through the grocery checkout unscathed.

Practicing small animal medicine is pretty safe; you just need to be mindful of what is going on around you and be diligent about good hygiene. As far as I can tell, I escaped getting any kind of zoonotic disease while in practice. I caught more germs from my kids when they were young!

* * * *

Afterthoughts by Dr Jefferson:

I agree with John and his emphasis on cleanliness which is so important in disease prevention. Today, however, not everyone agrees with vaccinations. Many don't realize how communicable viruses and bacteria are. The dog variant of rabies used to be a huge problem in the US for animals and people. The vaccine has pretty much eliminated that variant, and it's only the wild animal variant that we deal with now. It smolders in the woods in raccoons, foxes, etc. and every once in a while a person or domestic animal gets bitten.

Several years ago a number of horses in Maine died of Eastern Encephalitis, which is almost always fatal. Only unvaccinated horses got sick and died. No vaccinated horse even got sick. Vaccines work, and they work whether you believe in them or not.

# Dr Jefferson: Farm Animals and Epidemics

Joanie has an active show horse barn in Richmond, Maine. She called me one day, excited about her new purchase. She had just bought a yearling filly online—sight unseen. That's two "uh-ohs." The seller was in Georgia. I told Joanie to be sure the youngster was vaccinated for the common equine respiratory diseases at least two weeks before trucking. Too late. She had already been loaded with six others coming from three different farms in the Deep South. The truck was on its way to New England. I said, "Joanie, even if she gets off the truck looking healthy, be sure to isolate her from the herd for two weeks."

Joanie called when the filly arrived three days later. She said the horse was the picture of health so thought she'd be OK, and she turned her out with her herd. That was the third and biggest *uh-oh*. Her excitement was overriding her good sense. Love is a funny thing. Twenty-four hours later the filly stopped eating, ran a fever, and a thick nasal discharge began. All of Joanie's other horses were exposed. Over the next week most of her horses, also unvaccinated, got sick with what turned out to be Strangles. Strangles is an upper respiratory disease of horses that is extremely contagious and although rarely fatal, it does make horses very sick. It can take weeks for complete healing, and then the animal can still be a carrier for months beyond (although looking healthy). Sounds a little like Covid, doesn't it? Strangles is a reportable disease, so I was obligated to tell the state veterinarian. The Maine Department of Agriculture put the barn under quarantine until the last sick horse had totally recovered. The barn was shut down for a total of 12 weeks. No horses in. No horses out. No visitors. Total cost to Joanie: a few thousand dollars in vet bills and the loss of the year's show season.

Influenza is another respiratory disease in horses that will spread through barns with unvaccinated animals. Vaccines are also recommended against the mosquito borne encephalitis diseases.

The Covid pandemic of 2020 has lessons to teach us about disease prevention and transmission. Veterinarians are well trained in both. My veterinary career started with dairy cattle. Traditionally, cows are housed close to each other. This is also true for sheep. That causes problems when a contagious disease hits a farm. Social distancing is impossible so disease spreads rapidly. When a bug hits a barn, visitors should be barred.

Vets who travel from farm to farm have to be extra vigilant to avoid taking disease to the next place. The typical uniform for farm vets is a set of coveralls over regular clothes and rubber boots that come ¾ of the way to the knees. We always carry a stainless steel pail, a squirt bottle of disinfectant, and a long handled scrub brush. You learn the dance of scrubbing your boots without taking them off—toes, sides and heels. The sole surfaces are cleaned by balancing on one foot while cleaning the bottom of the other. Any object that carries disease is called a fomite. That includes our clothing, hands, and even our vehicles. No one wants to be a fomite. A vet with a reputation of being casual in moving from farm to farm soon would be out of business. Farm vets typically carry extra sets of clothing and coveralls in their trucks and may change frequently. If possible, we try to make the call to a farm with a disease, the last one of the day.

When horses are being trucked long distance, I try to persuade owners to have a vet at the farm of origin check them out before they leave and vaccinate them weeks before they depart. Face masks don't work on animals, so we depend on social distancing. New arrivals should unload in an isolated paddock at least 25 feet from other horses. For a period of two weeks disposable gloves should be worn when those animals are fed and handled. Hand washing and boot disinfecting are critical for personnel before returning to the main barn. No visitors should be permitted for two weeks, no matter how much an owner wants to show off the new acquisition. Here are some principals that veterinarians have learned both in school and on the job:

1. Vaccines that have been properly tested are amazingly effective. For example, in the large animal world, rabies, tetanus and encephalitis vaccines are close to 100% protective. Vaccines in human medicine have virtually eliminated smallpox and polio.

2. Approved disinfectants are excellent in sanitizing surfaces

against viruses and bacteria. When applied routinely, they slow disease spread.

3. Almost everything we learned from the Covid pandemic about vaccines and social distancing can be applied to livestock.

\* \* \* \*

Afterthoughts by Dr Hunt:

Viruses and bacteria don't care how much you love your animal, what kind of animal you have, or even your political and religious persuasion. Their purpose is to invade a host, replicate, and move onto the next, leaving the former host very sick or dead. Not very complicated. Since we can't see the little buggers, it's hard for us humans to grasp that viruses and bacteria are real, but we come up against them every day. Keeping them from attacking our pets and livestock is a lot more effective and cheaper than treating an infected beast. Veterinarians incorporate disease control as part of their job. Constant cleaning in my small animal vet hospital and Dave's use of overalls and boots aim for the same thing: keeping infectious agents from spreading from one animal to another. But animal owners must heed their vet's advice too. In Dave's story, Joanie didn't, and the horse and Joanie suffered the consequence.

Believe that viruses and bacteria exist and are dangerous. Trust your vet when he or she gives you advice on preventing diseases. We've got it down pretty good.

# Chapter 8
## Vets Cry, Too

## Dr Hunt: Veterinarians are Pet Owners, Too

Veterinarians have the reputation of being extraordinarily compassionate and loving to animals. We also shoulder the expectations from our clients that we both save their pets from deadly disease or injury, and also support their emotional needs during their pet's illness or euthanasia. It is a tall order to do both of these things simultaneously all the time. We must perform complex procedures in a professional manner and yet be compassionate at the same time. Maybe that is why there is a high suicide rate in my profession.

Have you ever thought about how veterinarians view their own pets? I can only speak for myself, but I loved my pets and gushed over them as much as anybody. After spending a day with someone else's pet, I still looked forward to reuniting with my dog or cat in the evening.

I adopted a cat right out of vet school that I called Shrimp because he was so small. He used to sit on my shoulder and peer into the sink when I washed the dishes. He must have had a fixation on liquids, because he also jumped onto my shoulder during dinner and then dived into a bowl of soup. He used to play with a ball at the end of an elastic string hanging from the doorway until he collapsed. In hindsight that should have been a clue he may have had an inherited heart condition. When I auscultated his heart the day I was to neuter him it sounded fine, but listening to a heart doesn't always reveal major problems. When I injected him with anesthesia in order to neuter him, his heart stopped immediately and he was gone—just like that. I went to the back of the vet hospital and cried. I kept this experience with me the rest of my veterinary career. Shrimp reminded me of how attached we get to our pets and how devastating it is to lose them at a young age and unexpectedly. I used that loss to help me empathize with future owners going through the same thing.

Sally, my golden retriever, was one of the best dogs I ever knew. She was sweet, gentle, happy, obedient, and loyal. She was great with the kids and simply loved being with the family. When she was six years old she seemed to be less energetic and she had lost a little weight. I brought her with me to my family's cabin in Trescott for a few days with my two brothers. My brothers noticed she seemed quiet and tired. When I got back to Bucksport I took an x-ray of Sally's abdomen because I felt a mass. As I suspected, she had a huge spleen. I removed it myself. I personally found it terrifying to operate on my own dog, but when you are one man practice you do what you gotta do. Miraculously, she survived the surgery—only one in five dogs survive that surgery. It turned out to be malignant. I wanted to do the best for Sally, so I started her on some chemotherapy. Unfortunately, the therapy was worse than the disease. She was weak, she vomited, and she didn't eat. I took her on our favorite walks but she couldn't finish them. My desire to do the very best backfired. I couldn't put her to sleep myself, so I left her at the clinic for my staff to do it. I literally flew out of the state the next morning for four or five days. I couldn't work. I loved her so much.

Veterinarians not only love all animals, but also they love their pets as much as anybody. Those emotions are personal and are kept private in a professional setting, though. My love for Shrimp and Sally and the sorrow and sadness of losing them gave me the empathy and understanding of how my clients felt when they lost their pets. I always drew from my own experience to help others get through their personal and private loss, never sharing my loss, only sharing my sincere condolences. We cry too; for our own pets and for our patients.

*  *  *  *

Afterthoughts by Dr Jefferson:

John's story of his cat, Shrimp, dying made my heart sink. Once I had a cow die when I gave her an injection meant to knock her out for just 20 minutes for a simple surgery. It happens. It's rare, and it's awful. It has to be doubly hard when you were the one that ended your own pet's life. I suspect it took John a long time to get over that. It's probably still there. Our anesthetics are so safe that these incidents are always unexpected. In most cases even a post mortem will not answer the question as to why. Unfortunately, like getting hurt by animals, it's part of the profession. I agree with John that such an experience gives us more compassion for the surprise loss that clients occasionally suffer.

# Dr Jefferson: My Deep Loss

Sometimes it's our own animal. That's when we appreciate all the pain our clients go through when faced with the reality of euthanasia.

I took on his care when he couldn't compete any more. He was Abe's favorite horse. Pat wasn't the strongest, the biggest, or the most handsome but when hooked up to a load, he always gave it his all. Abe had several draft horse teams. He used them on his place to work his fields. It wasn't that they were more efficient than tractors, but because they were alive and responsive to him. The purpose of the farm work was to get them in shape for pulling contests on the Maine fair circuit. That was Abe's real passion, finding two horses that worked well as a team and spending months getting them ready to take on the competition. A horse pull is an old country fair tradition very much alive in Maine. Two evenly matched horses pull a sled loaded with heavy blocks of concrete weights in front of an awed and enthusiastic crowd. Aging Pat no longer had the strength in his hind end that used to give Abe a little prize money and some big bragging rights.

"What are you planning to do with him?" I asked.

"Just keep him around I guess. The problem is he's happiest when he has a job. I don't want anyone else to pull him at the fairs. Those days are gone. I know it, and he knows it, but there are lots of guys who know Pat and would like to compete with him. I'm afraid if I sold him, he would get pushed too hard. He has the heart but not the strength. He might be abused and maybe embarrassed that he couldn't do it anymore."

"I have a wood lot, and I'd love to have him to pull out my firewood. Would you sell him to me?"

"Well," Abe paused. "You know, I really like Pat, and I'm not sure I'm ready to give him up. Why don't you just take him? Feed him and care for him, and when you are tired of him, I'll take him back. He'll always have a place on my farm."

"Done!" I was excited as I had long dreamed of having a horse to work in the woods.

Abe lent me an old harness, and Pat and I were in the wood business.

My equine hospital sat on 40 acres full of maples and oaks, some ready to be harvested. We had wood stoves both there and in my home, and went through 8 to 10 cords a year. Pat worked out well, and I enjoyed both the work and his easy manner. The only problem was the habit formed by years of competitive pulling. In those events the evener is dropped onto the iron hook on the front of the loaded sled, and it makes a loud clank. On hearing it, pulling horses are trained to throw themselves into the collar of their harness. The horse knows that if he takes off with a jerk he will have some momentum, and the regulation 27½-foot pull will be easier. Pat never worked that hard for me. I used him to haul sections of downed trees. I always kept the log to a manageable size, and the weight under a thousand pounds. In competition he used to pull five times that weight.

Initially, when I hooked him up and gave a little cluck, he would throw himself into his collar just like he did in the pulling ring. The load was so much lighter that Pat would trot off with it. There I was behind him, trying to keep up, pulling on the long reins to slow him down, tripping over wood slash in the way, trying to keep that log from running over me. A few times I had to jump over the log as it swung wildly. Eventually, Pat got the idea that this was slow steady work and not a herky-jerky horse pull. He learned, in time, to just lean into the collar and walk off slowly with the load.

They call drafts the gentle giants, and in general they are calmer than saddle horses. One day we had cousins visit us that were the same ages as our own kids. They wanted to meet Pat, so we went out to the barn. They patted his big legs and looked up at him in wonder as Pat, enjoying all the company, used his nose to muss their hair. Lots of giggles. The kids all wanted to get on his back. I lifted each of them up. We still have a photograph of all of them sitting in a line, legs far apart straddling his massive back. I gave the lead attached to his halter a little tug and said, "Come on, Pat, let's give the kids a ride." Horses are trained to follow you when you give a pull on the lead. It's important that you face the direction you are headed and not look at the horse. Facing the horse means you want him to stop. So I turned and starting walking ahead.

"Come on, Pat, let's go."

Pat didn't move. I gave a stronger tug. No reaction. I turned and looked back. One of the kids had slipped off Pat's back and lay on the ground, her head just in front of one of his front feet. Pat knew she was there, and wasn't about to take a step, no matter how hard I pulled.

I had Pat for about a year. One day I was an hour away when my pager went off. I called, and Kim, my veterinary technician, said, "I think you better come home. It's Pat. He's down in his paddock."

"Lying down? Outside? He's never done that."

"I know. David, I think his leg is broken."

I drove home, paying no attention to speed limits. I felt like I had swallowed a rope that was tied in a tight knot deep down in my belly. I pulled into the yard and saw Pat lying on his side. His head came up slightly when I approached and then eased back down. There was a massive swelling high on his hind leg. I picked up his foot and slowly swung his leg forward. There was a grating of bone on bone, and again, his head lifted. In my career as a horse doctor I had seen this before. He had a complete fracture of the femur, the biggest bone in the body. He must have slipped, twisted that leg under him and fallen on it, snapping it in two. Given the size of the horse and the severity of the fracture, there was nothing to be done. Kim drew out two syringes full of euthanasia solution. I bit my cheek to keep the knot in my stomach under control and not up in my throat where it would open the floodgates. It was like Pat not to react as I slipped the large needle into his jugular vein and slowly pushed the plunger. It was so hard to do—killing this big hunk of horse I had grown to love. Within the hour I called Abe and told him what had happened.

I'm sure he could hear in my voice all the emotion I was trying to stuff back down. He heard me out and said, "It's just one of those things that happens. I know he enjoyed his stay with you. Do you mind burying him there for me?"

"I'll take care of that, Abe. I'm so sorry."

It hits hard when, with no warning, you lose an animal whose company you have enjoyed. You don't fully realize how important they are to you until it happens. One minute they are okay and next, gone. It hurts every time you walk by that empty stall or the cold dog bed. It's been many years, but sometimes I still think about and miss old Pat. He learned, along with me, that you don't have to throw yourself into the collar quite so hard. You can ease into some of life's loads and find to your surprise that you can often walk off with them. I have thought about the hundreds of horses I have put down, their owners in tears standing with me. Standing there, watching Pat breathing his last, I learned that vets cry too.

(This chapter was edited from Dr Jefferson's book on equine euthanasia, *Goodbye Old Friend*)

\* \* \* \*

Afterthoughts by Dr Hunt:

Dave's personal journey with Pat is heart wrenching and yet inspiring on so many levels. He loved and learned from Pat, had the professional strength to euthanize Pat himself (which I guarantee you is one hell of a thing to do as a vet), and accepted his own grief, which helped him help his clients in similar situations.

Your vet is a person just like you. We have animals in our own lives that we love and go ga-ga over, just like you. Dave and I thought sharing our personal stories of loss and how we felt could give you a better appreciation of who veterinarians are as fellow pet owners and maybe encourage you to give us a break if we seem off on some days.

# Chapter 9
## OOPS

## Dr Hunt: A Slip of the Scalpel and Other Mishaps

You never want to hear a jeweler say "Oops!" while cutting your grandmother's diamond ring, or hear your surgeon whisper "Oops" under their breath during a procedure. Vets are only human, and we work on living creatures that are unique and unpredictable. I dare say every vet has had one or more *oops* moments. You do the best you can, follow the procedures that were taught to you, and still things happen. Some are beyond your control, some happen because of a lapse in concentration or from an instant decision due to extenuating circumstances, and some are just bad luck. Losing an animal, whether it was your fault or not, is an awful feeling that you can't shake. You bring it home, you bring it to bed, you wake up thinking about it—it's always in the back of your mind. Veterinarians are expected to be perfect. Pet owners assume we are, and veterinarians try to live up to those expectations.

I wasn't in practice very long when I had a major Oops moment. It was my fault and shouldn't have happened, thus qualifying it as a *genuine* oops. In my second year as a practicing vet, I was performing a surgery on a large old dog with a perineal hernia. These hernias are relatively rare. I would see maybe one or two every couple of years. What happens is the musculature around the rectum becomes thin, and eventually a hole or opening develops between the rectum and thigh muscles. When the dog defecates, it puts pressure in the rectal area, pushing internal organs out through the hernia. The most common organ to squeeze through is the colon, but I've seen bladders and even small intestines squeeze through. The owner usually brings in their dog because they see a big bulge under or next to the anus that may change in size. The goal of the surgery is to put everything back into the abdomen and sew up the hole. Not as easy as it sounds.

Sometimes these hernias go unnoticed, so herniated material can develop adhesions and scar tissue, virtually cementing them into place outside the body. In these cases, part of the surgery is to dissect all the adhesions and identify and free up any organs like the colon so they can be shoved back into the abdomen before closing the hernia up. This particular dog's bladder had come out, and it looked like it had been there for a while. I was amazed the dog could actually pee. The hernia was a mess. I could recognize the bladder, but the connective tissue, adhesions, and muscles were all blended together. As I was trying to dissect the bladder free so I could press it back into the body, I saw a cord-like structure wrapped around the bladder. Thinking it was a tendon or part of a non-functioning muscle, I cut it. It took me a few seconds to realize what I had done. The inside of the cord was hollow with a very smooth, glistening inner lining. Holy cow, I cut the urethra! No way around it, I had to sew it back together, but first I had to free up the bladder and the urethra and get them back into the abdomen. I then went into the abdomen via a new large incision in the abdomen. The urethra was not flexible enough for me to exteriorize the two ends and work on it outside the body (which would make it easier to sew up). I had to sew it up in the abdomen. I put a catheter through the urethra from the penis and ran through both ends. Three hours later it was reattached. I was sweating bullets the whole time, and my boss' tactic was to steer clear. He never came back to check or hover. I was on my own. Fortunately, the urethra inner lining heals very quickly, but my fear was it would spring a leak. The dog stayed in the hospital for a few days with the catheter in place to give the sutured ends time to heal. It did heal and the dog eventually went home, bladder in place, and urinating to beat the band.

  In my early years in Bucksport I was trying to remove a large mass from the throat of a dog. The dog was lying on its back, head back, neck stretched out. The neck is a very busy place. Large blood vessels like the jugular and the carotids run up through the neck. Major nerves snake through the area as well. Aggressive tumors don't care about such things. They grow on, over, and even through body parts and have the gumption to force the host to feed them with their own blood vessels. Dissecting one of those suckers is a slow, painstaking process. Avoiding blood vessels is your number one priority. Unfortunately, my scalpel nicked a major vessel. To this day I'm not sure which one, but it didn't matter because when I nicked it, a fountain of blood arose from the neck like a Phoenix and hit the ceiling! Fran, my loyal and fantastic tech, was

## Dog and Pony Show

by my side witnessing Old Faithful. The ceiling, the dog, the table and we were covered in blood in a matter of seconds. I grabbed a handful of surgical gauzes and slapped them over the gushing vessel. Then I asked Fran to hold on to the gauze so I could get a needle and suture. Time was of the essence. The dog could bleed out in a matter of minutes. So we did a tag team approach. I would yell, "NOW," Fran would lift the gauze, and for a split second I could visualize the lacerated vessel. During that split second, I tried to place the suture around the vessel. It took several tries, but I finally tied off the vessel. Then I still had to remove the mass. It took forever, and we feared another volcano eruption of blood the whole time. Needless to say, we had a lot of cleaning to do. By the way, the dog went home none the worse for wear. Now that is an OOPS moment!

On the lighter side, I've had a number of minor mishaps during my tenure as a vet, like sticking a vaccination needle out the other end of the tented skin and squirting vaccine onto the table, or sticking myself with a needle as I was trying to remove the needle guard (as a side note, I found that even a small needle prick led to excessive bleeding that only a BandAid could control, putting a Kleenex on it for a half minute did not cut it).

One time I got very involved in expressing anal glands on a dog and I leaned over to see what I was doing. Apparently my concentration caused me to open my mouth, and suddenly the glands let loose and squirted into my mouth! Another time I thought the owner asked me to check his dog's rear. As I was putting on gloves and then lifting the tail the client spoke up, "Uh Doc, I said, 'check the ear'."

While neutering a cat, the stitch that tied off the spermatic cord and blood vessel slipped as I released the knotted cord. As it retreated into the body, blood was shooting out at me. Nothing I could do. Fortunately, the blood clotted, but the cat had a blood clot the size of an orange sticking out from under its tail.

Female dogs rarely mess with their incisions from a spay, but I had an exception. I did a routine spay on a large German Shepherd in the morning. That afternoon, the head surgery tech came running into the office to tell me the dog chewed out all the stitches and her intestines came out and she ate some of her intestines. That was a long afternoon of stitching up intestines and sewing her back up. Needless to say. I put an E-collar on her afterwards.

I've also had a reverse oops. I neutered a Great Dane, and two weeks later the owner claimed I didn't take out both testicles. Post-surgically neutered dogs can have a reaction that causes the empty scrotal sac to fill with fluid. The fluid can harden, and I think the owner saw the hardened fluid and convinced themselves I didn't do the job. I know I can count to two, so I tried to tell them I took out both. They insisted I go back in. I obliged, with the agreement that they pay for it if there was no testicle. When they came to pick up the dog after my exploratory surgery, I gave them the bill.

Oops moments are far and few between, but they are the ones you remember. I did surgery on literally 1000s of pets, and 98% did just fine. Owners, understandably, take our skill for granted. They just assume their pet is in good hands. It's called trust, and I valued client trust more than anything.

\* \* \* \*

Afterthoughts by Dr Jefferson:

Don't we hate our oops moments! We are serious about our tasks and then, right when you don't want or expect it, we get handed one of life's surprises. John's oops moments seemed to be mostly at surgeries. Even when everything is going your way, surgery is never a relaxing activity. Throw in an oops, and for a few moments you want to be anywhere else. Then you fight the panic as everything unravels, and you gut it out. Oops times are always unexpected, but they do make interesting stories. Sometimes, years later, we can even laugh. Sometimes.

# Dr Jefferson: My Mistake

Any vet who that tells you they can't quickly recall mistakes they've made is either not very truthful, or not very busy. We all make them, and if our error makes us lose sleep, that's the one we never make again. This mistake came after I owned my own practice, and it was the cause for many sleepless nights.

I was looking at a lame horse named Bobby for a new client, Ann. Lameness work is part of every equine vet's day. We each have our own procedure for these exams and do things in the same order each time so we don't miss anything. I watched Bobby move at a trot. He was favoring his right front leg. Instead of landing flat he was landing toe first, which made me think the problem was in the heel of that foot.

Part of the equipment for a thorough lameness exam is a set of hoof testers. These look like giant pliers and enable the examiner to put pressure on areas of the foot to see if you can get the horse to say "ouch". Bobby had no reaction to the testers. Palpation of the rest of the leg didn't reveal any problems, so I turned my attention back to his foot. To insure that this was the issue, I decided to perform a nerve block. This means injecting a local anesthetic around the nerves of the foot to see if that will temporarily make the horse sound. If you have ever had dental surgery, you know that this numbing is usually very effective.

Nerve blocking anesthetics all have the same "aine" ending or sound to their name. For example, you may be familiar with Novocain, a brand name, which incidentally has not been available for many years but has become a generic name for this type of drug. My go to anesthetic was Lidocaine. I took a bottle from my truck and injected three cc over the paired nerves going to the back of Bobby's foot. I waited five minutes and then used a ball point pen to test the area for sensitivity. He felt my little pokes, so I waited five minutes and then tried again. I was surprised that he still had feeling, so I pulled up a few more cc and reinjected the area. This time I waited ten minutes and retested him. Bobby still felt every prick of my pen, and was getting agitated and hard to handle. Ann was having a hard time controlling him. Part of my mistake that day was not having a tech with me.

I have always made it a point to use medications before their expiration dates. I checked the label, and it was still a year from outdating. I told Ann that I'd never had this happen before. Lidocaine is a very reliable drug. Bobby should not have had any sensation in his foot. I picked up the bottle again and looked carefully at its label. My head started to pound, and my internal voice cried, "Oh, no! Tell me it's not true!" I had picked up a bottle of the same size and color, produced by the same company. It was not Lidocaine. I had been injecting the horse with epinephrine. Epinephrine is another name for adrenalin, secreted naturally by the adrenal glands. It's the hormone that makes your heart race and gets you ready to fight or run. No wonder Bobby was getting agitated.

I didn't want to say the words but knew I had to.

"Oh Ann, I'm afraid I made a mistake." I explained what I had done. She asked if there might be side effects. I replied, "Yes, he's apt to get even more excited in the next half hour."

I called a vet friend with more experience. Fortunately, he picked up. It wasn't very reassuring when he said this could cause a real issue. I said, holding the phone tightly to my ear and glancing at the owner, "What would that be?" He reminded me that the epinephrine might cause a necrosis of the injected area. He was right. Epinephrine can cause constriction of local blood vessels. He suggested flooding the area I had injected with saline to dilute the epinephrine and its possible side effects. Since Bobby was getting harder and harder to handle, I gave an IV tranquilizer and then injected as much saline as the skin could contain. His lower leg looked like a fat sausage when I was done. Ann was understandably confused by all this. As I apologized to her, in my head I could hear Dr Erb, my first boss, saying, "If you can't help them, for God's sake, don't do anything to hurt them." I had done just that.

It was a week before I got a good night's sleep, blaming myself over and over for my carelessness.

Before I left Ann, I showed her the two bottles and told her how bad I felt. I said there would be no charge for the morning's work and told her if Bobby had any aftereffects, I would take care of it. She was quiet and said that she understood. I imagined a law suit coming on like a runaway freight train. I called her every few days, and after two weeks it was clear that Bobby would have no ill effects. Had all this happened to an established client I'm sure I would have been forgiven. However, that was the one and only time I saw Ann or her horse Bobby. I was never invited back.

I made some rules as a result of that day that my techs and I strictly followed from then on:

1. Always keep same size bottles from the same manufacturer in different places on the truck.

2. Keep bottles of epinephrine in their own plastic case.

3. Read and reread the entire label on every bottle picked up, every time, without exception.

\* \* \* \*

Afterthoughts by Dr Hunt:

The "oops" moments Dave and I had in our careers may have been with completely different animals, but the emotions were the same. A sense of failure, letting people down, questioning one's veterinary skills, and shame all combined to cause sleepless nights and anxious days. I'm not sure our readers can empathize, and I mean that in a kind way. You really have to be in our shoes as veterinarians. Telling you of our "oops" moments gives you an accurate picture of veterinary medicine. It's not all petting puppies or being out in a pasture on a beautiful spring day helping with lambing. Our profession is full of surprises with many gratifying triumphs and agonizing defeats, and I would do it again in a heartbeat.

# Chapter 10
## Final Goodbye

# Dr Hunt: Peaceful Death

It was a busy afternoon at the clinic. I was double booked. Lame dogs, itchy cats, vomiting, diarrhea—a typical day at the office. At around four o'clock, I stepped out of the exam room into the front desk area, and I noticed the waiting rooms were empty. I knew immediately what was about to happen. A client was bringing their dog in to be euthanized. My staff cleared the schedule to give the owners some sense of privacy. This dog and his owners were especially close to me, and my staff knew I would not be in any shape to see any more patients for the rest of the day.

The dog was a very old Shih Tzu that was diabetic, arthritic, blind, had bilateral cruciate ruptures in the knees, and was going into kidney failure. The owners were an elderly couple that lived across the street from me in town. My wife and I went over to their house on Friday nights to have wine and hors d'oeuvres and play Wii Golf. They loved their dog, but knew it was not fair to keep him alive. Pat was a man who lived to make his wife, Patty, happy, but he couldn't do anything about this. Patty was a wreck. She was so distraught she couldn't talk or even recognize where she was. The Shih Tzu, Sammy, was decompensating rapidly. He was thin, weak, dehydrated, and barely aware of his surroundings, but did manage to wag his tail when Patty spoke to him. I injected the solution in the leg vein quickly and smoothly while they held him. He relaxed and went limp within seconds. I checked his heart and told them they could be with him as long as they needed, and I excused myself to give them privacy (I actually excused myself to go into my office and cry). My wife gave them a special rose bush in his honor, and they planted it in their front yard.

That was an especially emotional euthanasia, but really there were no cavalier, unemotional euthanasias. Whether it's a dog, a cat, or a mouse, losing a pet hurts. Some people hide their emotions, some wear them on their sleeve, but all people grieve. It is an unwritten assumption that their veterinarian will perform a smooth, painless, peaceful euthanasia. As veterinarians, we are expected to act professionally to get the job done in a seamless way, show honest empathy, and convey sorrow for the owner's loss. That takes a lot out of you, believe me.

Often owners of multi-pet households asked me if the surviving pets would grieve or even notice their buddy missing. I unequivocally said yes. It has been documented that pets do indeed grieve over the loss of a fellow pet. At first the surviving pet will notice a lack of presence and will experience a change in their typical day, resulting in confusion, withdrawal, inappetence, and inappropriate vocalization. They were so used to playing, sleeping, and eating with their deceased buddy that they literally can't function without their old companion. I told clients that pets can grieve up to six weeks. Oddly, an animal will overcome their grief literally overnight. Whatever internal process is going on, grief resolution has an off switch. I've had many clients come in to report that their dog was grieving for weeks, then suddenly one morning it started acting like nothing happened. Numerous cat owners reported to me that their surviving cat would wander around the house moaning and crying aimlessly for weeks then suddenly stop.

I do have one odd story to share. A client told me she pulled her refrigerator out from the wall to clean behind it. When sweeping behind the fridge, she swept out a bunch of hair from her dog that had passed away the year before. When the surviving dog came over to sniff the pile of hair, dust, and dirt, it began to howl and cry uncontrollably. It couldn't be consoled. She had to quickly sweep the pile into a bag and throw it in the outside garbage can. Only then the dog stopped yowling.

For me, euthanasia was a double-edged sword. I knew I was helping relieve an animal from suffering and helping the owners deal with the situation, but I was also emotionally invested. I was ending a life, which is contrary to what I'm supposed to do as a vet, and it was important to show true sorrow and empathy to the owner. That takes a lot of emotional energy, and after 32 years of doing that I was ready to pass that part of my job over to younger vets.

*\*\*\*\**

Afterthoughts by Dr Jefferson:

John's reflection about euthanasia is well thought out and well written. I am in total agreement. My additional statement is that euthanasia of your animal at the right time should be a partnership decision made by you and your veterinarian after considering all the options. It can be the right choice.

# Dr Jefferson: Old Red

Red turned 28 in the spring. For the past ten years the Bensons called him Old Red. If we can judge such things, Red had a good life. When family stuff got intense, Red would get a visit from one of them to tell him all about it. He never offered an opinion. He always listened.

Over the past year Red had started to fail. His teeth were close to the gum line. Chewing even the leafiest hay was difficult. Despite twice a day mashes fortified with extra carbs and fat, he was losing muscle mass. Cataracts were compromising his vision. At night he would occasionally bump into the walls of his stall. It was mid-October, and the family realized that his time had come. I was asked to lay him away before the ground was frozen. He was to be buried out back by the stone wall, near the old field pine, next to two of the family dogs. We all knew it was his time and the right thing to do. He might have made it through one more winter, but likely not.

Ed and Mary felt it important to talk to their children about Red and to invite them into the decision and the process. They left it up to each child whether to be present or not. Then, on that chilly October day, Mary led Red out of the barn. Red had become noticeably weak. Ed walked behind and a little to Red's side, holding his tail to steady him. All four of their kids followed us out. I remember being impressed by the respect they demonstrated with no prompting. It was like they were walking into church. There was no fooling around. They walked several feet behind Red. When they talked to each other, it was in whispers. As Mary approached the spot the family had picked out, she slowed down and then stopped. Red, always accommodating, slowed and stopped by her side.

Here, near other old family pets, we were at the spot where Red would be buried. Neither Mary nor Ed had ever had a horse euthanized, and, like the kids, had no idea what to expect. I asked Erin, my long time technician, to take Red's lead shank from Mary. I explained that Erin had been through this many times and that I depended on her to keep us all safe.

I made eye contact with each of the kids. "While Red is still with us, let's take this chance to say goodbye and thank him for all the good years he has given us. Then, when you're finished, I'm going to ask you all to move back. We don't know which way he's going to fall, and we don't want to get in the way of that."

Mary bit off a piece of the apple she had been carrying, and Red's lips gently took it from her hand. Each of the children went up to Red, stroked his nose or patted his shoulder.

"Good bye, Red; I'll miss you."

"I love you, Red."

Two of the youngest just hugged his front leg and whispered a secret goodbye. Each of them moved back as I had asked.

"Everyone OK?" They nodded.

Red didn't flinch as I injected a tranquilizer into the left jugular vein on his neck. Within a minute his eyes lost their focus, and his head started to drop. I waited another two minutes for complete sedation and then injected 50 cc of the euthanasia solution into his vein. With her free hand, Erin handed me a second full syringe to follow the first.

Thirty-seconds later, Red took a deep breath, his tired old legs gave way, and he slowly sank to the ground. His breathing stopped. Erin knelt down by his head and stroked his cheek. No one spoke. Another half minute and Red surprised the family by taking one last, very deep breath. His penis slipped slowly out of its sheath, and a pint of urine flowed out over his leg onto the ground.

I moved in between Red's front and rear legs, crouched down near his rib cage, and placed my stethoscope into my ears and listened for his heart. The beats came slower and slower. Lub dub. Lub…dub, Lub ... dub, lub ..., and then it was quiet. I glanced at Erin and nodded. She touched his cornea with her finger. There was no reflex eyelid movement. Red was gone.

(This chapter was edited from Dr Jefferson's book on equine euthanasia, *Goodbye Old Friend*)

\* \* \* \*

Dr John H. Hunt and Dr David A. Jefferson

Afterthoughts by Dr Hunt:

Veterinarians take an oath to care for animals and prevent suffering. That includes ending a life when suffering and pain cannot be controlled or the quality of life is poor.

Euthanizing an animal is part of our job, and a very important one. We not only spare the animal from suffering, but also we help the farmer or pet owner with the decision, perform the euthanasia, help take care of the body, and console the owner in appropriate ways. Dave and I may have approached clients differently, but our empathy and understanding were similar. That is why Dave's other book, *Goodbye, Old Friend,* can be read by all animal lovers, not just horse people. This is another part of veterinary medicine people tend to overlook. We love animals so much that we understand the importance of euthanasia in helping to relieve animals of suffering—and the public depends on us to do it compassionately and professionally. There were many times I talked with a youngster who loved animals and wanted to be a vet, until they realized they couldn't bear putting an animal to sleep. One needs to respect animals as well as love them in order to be a vet.

# Chapter 11
## Wake Up Call

# Dr Hunt: My Big Injury that Threatened My Practice

As I described in a previous chapter, practicing veterinary medicine can be dangerous. Getting attacked, scratched, or bitten is no laughing matter—and it hurts! I discovered very quickly how to treat my injuries to avoid infection or a visit to the doctor. I never missed a day of work from a bite or scratch. As a matter of fact, in the 32 years of practicing, I may have missed two or three days of work due to illness. But there was one time I was almost knocked out of working for weeks, if not months.

I bet you're thinking I'm going to tell you a whopper of a tale about a big dog attacking me. Sorry to disappoint you but the injury didn't even happen at the veterinary hospital. It happened on a basketball court, but the consequence was potentially a game changer for my business.

On Sunday evenings I used to get together with a bunch of local guys for a pick-up basketball game at the school gym. Our group was an interesting mix, including the fire chief, police captain and detective, workers from the paper mill and even a radio sports broadcaster. It was a great time to hang out with other guys since my staff were all women. We were all mediocre, slow, and bad shots, and fouling each other was part of the game. We got to run around, get sweaty, pretend to play basketball, and have fun. Everyone had their own playing personality. One guy, who was not tall but was built like a tank, was known to plow right down the middle like a bull in a China shop. I usually stepped aside when I was in his path, since attempting to draw a charging foul would be suicide. And besides, we rarely called fouls even if we needed to treat a bloody nose or get help picking ourselves off the floor (all in good fun, mind you). Another guy was always putting his joints back in place. During the game he would come up lame. We would halt the game as he went to the sidelines to twist an ankle or knee back into joint, or slam his shoulder against the wall to replace his dislocated shoulder. I exaggerate a little, but that is how it seemed. Another guy was very clever and stayed under the radar. He was the oldest of the group, and apparently with age came wisdom. He would jog up and down the court and sneak around to get open. Another guy was on the police force and younger than the rest; he had played basketball in high school. He had a terrific 15-foot jumper that was indefensible. Then there was me. I was the guy running around the court like a mad man trying to get free, or dribbling the ball around trying to pass it off. I wasn't any worse than anyone else, I just looked kind of manic.

Well, one Sunday when we were gathering at the gym, four teenagers showed up. They were the kids of the older guys and their friends. I looked at this as an opportunity to prove to myself, that at 45, I was still young and indestructible and could keep up with these punks. Intellectually, I knew my reflexes and general ability were far inferior to those kids, but my ego swept all that aside. Facts be damned, I'd run rings around those youngsters. Well, I couldn't and didn't. A kid was dribbling up to me as I was backing up trying to defend him. He gave me a head fake and dribbled past me. I reacted, but not fast enough, and I tripped over his feet as he fled by for a layup. I fell so quickly I couldn't bring my hands out to break the fall, and I landed on my right shoulder. A searing sharp pain came from my shoulder. When I picked myself up, I tried to assess the damage. The pain was so bad I didn't want to move the shoulder an inch. I thought I had dislocated it. It occurred to me that I could simply go over to the wall and slam it back in. After all, I saw my friend do it a number of times, but when I put my hand over my shoulder I felt something crunching. I realized slamming against the wall was not an option. I've felt crunching like that in my patients after a car accident. Something was broken. No more basketball that night or for a long time afterward.

A friend drove me home. I spent the evening with an ice pack on my shoulder, ibuprofen in my blood, and a mind that was trying to figure out what to do about work the next morning. After a very poor night's sleep, I put my arm in a makeshift sling and off I went to work as if it was just another day. As long as my arm was in the sling and I didn't move it I was okay. Seeing animals was a trial to say the least. I needed my clients or techs to restrain my patients. I had to get creative with giving vaccinations. Fortunately, it was my right shoulder that was injured, and I am a lefty. I would lean over the pet, grab the scruff of the neck with my right hand that was in a sling, and inject with my left. The cats were a bit nervous. They weren't used to Dr Hunt getting so up close and personal during a shot. I could see their ears twitch back when I approached, a sure sign of apprehension.

By that afternoon I finally called my personal physician, Bill. He had been my doctor for years and appreciated and respected my vocation. He recommended I go to the emergency room. I flatly said, "No, why should I? I'm doing fine, I just need you to evaluate what I think is a fractured collar bone." He relented with a chuckle and told me to come in Tuesday for an x-ray. I normally took Tuesday afternoons off, so I zipped up to Bangor, got an x-ray, and shortly thereafter was sitting in Bill's office looking at my distal fracture of the collar bone. He felt that 8 to 12 weeks rest in a sling would allow that kind of fracture to heal properly. At first I was relieved. No surgery and therefore no time away from work. Then I got a shiver up my spine. Work! What was I going to do?

For the next 12 weeks I attended to my patients in a sling. My clients were very sympathetic and helpful. Of course some had to rib me about where pretending I was a high schooler had gotten me, but I straightened up and looked proud and wore my sling as a Red Badge of Courage.

Surgery days were another story. I resigned myself that one handed surgery was not in the best interest of my patients, although the leaning over technique did allow me to perform basic surgeries. I could neuter dogs and cats, spay cats, and remove most lumps, but I could not spay dogs. I needed both hands to do part of that surgery. My staff turfed off surgery cases to my sympathetic, understanding colleagues in the surrounding towns.

Without the help of my staff, I couldn't have pulled it off. I didn't miss a day's work, I just had a lot of very uncomfortable cats during office calls. As for basketball. That is a young man's game even though us old guys continue to try and fulfill our second childhood playing it. We never learn. The fear of losing weeks or months of work in my one-man practice scared me away from basketball for a few years. I did return several times, but it wasn't the same. The fear of an awkward rebound rupturing my ACL or coming down on my ankle distracted me from having a good time. I decided I best leave basketball to the youngsters and my old fellow teammates who continued to charge the basket with abandon and replace dislocated joints while running down the court.

* * * *

Afterthoughts by Dr Jefferson:

Ouch! I could feel my shoulder go when John hit the floor! Pretty tough guy, not missing a day of work. He was the only vet in his practice and so he had to show up, as handicapped as he was. Payroll is always waiting. Three months in a sling had to be difficult. He didn't mention the discomfort he must have felt during healing. I'm sure that even turning in bed was painful. Certainly this story underlines how important good veterinary technicians are to a practice. John and I have a strong appreciation for techs. When we are handicapped in some way, we have both been surprised at how they are always ready and willing to pitch in and do what needs to be done.

# Dr Jefferson: Big Doors Swing on Small Hinges

W Clement Stone was a highly successful businessman and author. The quote about the big doors came from him. Compared to the size and bulk of a door, a hinge is a tiny thing. The idea is that little events in our lives—the hinges—can have a huge influence on what happens from then on.

One small hinge for me was a conversation that took place in a horse barn at the Cumberland, Maine, fairgrounds 30 years ago. Housed in this stable were four Standardbred racehorses. They were owned and cared for by Bob and Helen Gossom who were both retired. Looking after and racing their horses was the way the couple spent their days. It was something they enjoyed and did together. Their home was a house trailer right on the grounds of the track. Their horses were more a hobby than a business. Every once in a while one of their horses would beat the competition and come in first, second or third. That's all it took to keep Helen and Jim excited and showing up every day. I liked working for the couple as they truly loved their animals and were appreciative clients. At that time the majority of my practice was with Standardbreds. When I bought the practice, that's how it was and seemed like it was going to stay, until the day that a small hinge, just a little remark from Helen, shut one door and opened another.

I always stopped at the Gossom barn as part of my rounds at the race track. That day, as usual, I backed my practice truck up to the big barn doors and got out to see if their horses were in need of anything. That's the way it works in veterinary practice at a racetrack. Appointments are rare. You just show up on a certain day and make the rounds. I was just greeting Helen when another horse trainer walked up to the barn and said,

"Doc, I got one goin' tonight and he's in over his head. Can you mix me up a little something to help him out?" He was asking for a pre-race medication. A little explanation here is necessary. A pre-race is a syringe full of a mixture of various injectable vitamins, minerals, hormones, and sometimes steroids to make a race horse more competitive on race day. It has the potential of helping a horse that is sore or perhaps lacking stamina or courage. The idea is to give them a competitive edge. This particular horseman had his horses on his farm but knew where to find me. He was asking me to load up a syringe with what I thought would help his horse that night. When he got home, he would give it to his horse a few hours before the race. I filled a syringe for him from a few different vials. I asked him for ten dollars, which he swapped with me for the medication. No receipt requested or given. The Alexander Hamilton went into my pocket.

 I have to pause here to explain the pre-race medication situation. In some racing jurisdictions certain medications are allowed on race day. In others they are forbidden. At this particular time there was a— no medication on race day— rule in Maine. This was largely ignored by both trainers, owners, and, I'm embarrassed to say, most vets, including me. It was a common belief that horses would do better with a little help. The crucial question then, as today, was not whether the medication was legal, but rather, would it show in a drug test. Drug tests from urine or a blood sample are always taken from the winner of a race, or may be pulled from any horse that the racing steward designates. Perhaps you remember Lance Armstrong, who was quite sophisticated in self-medicating before he mounted his bicycle. He was always one step ahead of the drug testers. The horse racing scene I knew was kind of like that. It may be not be legal, but this or that drug doesn't show on testing, so it's OK. Wink. Wink. So, true confession: I knew exactly what would pass the drug test and what wouldn't. I wasn't proud of it then, and I now regret my involvement in the practice. At the time I felt that if I didn't to it, someone else would. A poor excuse for anything that is inexcusable. Plain and simple, the practice is cheating.

 So, back to my story. This trainer who asked for a little help to take home to his horse made the request openly, in front of Bob and Helen who were standing there with me.

 After he left with the syringe in his pocket Helen said, "David, can I ask you a question?"

 "Sure, Helen."

 "That pre-race that you dispensed for that horse, was that for the horse's good, or for that trainer's?"

I kept a straight face, but I felt like she had just stuck a spear into my chest. I knew that her question was not only legitimate, but was an indictment of my behavior within the veterinary profession. When I left the track that day, I knew that I couldn't live with myself if I continued in the same way. A very little hinge moved, and the door started swinging that day.

I believe God has a way of honoring right decisions. Within a week a friend of mine, who had a solid equine practice working on saddle horses, called to say she wanted to meet for lunch. Over a sandwich a few days later I was flabbergasted when she handed me a list of names. She had made a decision to retire from practice and was recommending me to her clientele. As a result I was able to leave the race track and concentrate on sport and backyard horses for my income. I said goodbye to the track and never returned. Within a year my income was not only equal to previous levels but continued to grow, and I had to hire more veterinarians to help with the load.

I was guilty of bending the rules in a culture where it was tolerated. Helen Gossom, with a simple question, brought the truth home to me. After all the winks and excuses, it all comes down to just this: Do the right thing.

* * * *

Afterthoughts by Dr Hunt:

David's Wake Up Call was one of integrity, honesty and professionalism. He is a consummate veterinarian. Honest, hardworking, caring, and truly wanting to do the right thing the best way he knows how. He found himself on the wrong side of vet medicine in the Standardbred Horse racing culture. Admitting to himself he was doing the wrong thing and doing something about it was a lot more courageous than me dealing with a broken shoulder. I hope his clients realized they had a jewel of a horse vet in David. Kudos to my friend, colleague, and fellow author.

# Chapter 12
## Funny Stories

## Dr Hunt: Finding Humor in My Job

Humor got me through the day at work. Treating sick and injured animals takes a lot of concentration and can be emotionally draining. Seeing the lighter side of things helped relieve the tension. Let me share some humorous vet hospital vignettes that helped lighten my emotional load.

Every morning Ben, my Border Collie, would sit at the door as I got ready to leave for work. He would be underfoot as I walked to the car, and would automatically jump into the back seat and sit like a human so he could look out the window, seemingly taking note of everything going by. He reminded me of commuters taking the train into New York City, staring out the window, watching the world go by. The only difference was that Ben left a nose print on the car window.

When we arrived at work he would dutifully run into my office and promptly curl up under my desk—and there he would stay until lunch. At least I thought he did. One morning doughnuts were brought in by a staff member, probably because they anticipated a rough day ahead. I get very excited about doughnuts, so I grabbed one right away, knowing that once office calls started, I would be tied up for a few hours and the doughnuts would be gone. I didn't get any special treatment even though I was the boss. I took my stash and squirreled it away on my desk in my office. When some free time opened up, I ran to my office with my coffee, my mouth watering in anticipation of a jelly doughnut—but the doughnut was gone. The wrapper was on the floor near my desk. Ben was under the desk looking like he was sleeping. Yeah, right! When I let out a loud expletive, Ben squeezed his eyes tight. He had jumped up onto the desk, stolen my doughnut, and licked the wrapper clean. As with all thieves, he left evidence behind on the floor and had a guilty countenance. Lucky for me there were some doughnuts left, but Ben's office antics didn't always turn out so well. One morning, my associate left his lunch on top of his desk. I forgot to tell him about Ben's secret life as a thief. Ben treated himself to a big old ham sandwich and some cookies, much to the chagrin of my associate.

Ben wasn't the only critter who got up to mischief in my office. I had a client who rehabilitated and fostered porcupines—aptly named the Porcupine Lady. She was a middle-aged woman who wore a handwoven stocking hat down over her ears, with unwashed hair sticking out the back. She wore a long, ratty coat and fingerless gloves. She didn't talk much, but it was clear she loved her porcupines. One day, she brought in a porc that had an abscess on its stomach. Handling porcupines is not that hard as long as they are calm (and gloves help). The Porcupine Lady put on welders' gloves to tip the porc onto its back so I could check the lesion. I excused myself to go to my pharmacy to find some ointment. Apparently, I left the exam door open because as I was looking at my pharmacy, I caught some movement on the floor out of the corner of my eye. I quickly turned to see the porcupine waddling towards me at a fairly good clip, for a porcupine, that is. For a second, I didn't know what to do. Here were 1000s of quills walking towards me and I didn't have any way to stop them. I yelled for the Porcupine Lady, and she ran around the corner from the exam room, welders' gloves on, and scooped the porc up. She was smirking as she picked up the porc. She commented that she thought the porc liked me. I was not flattered. That porc's brethren had gotten me out of bed many times to pull quills out of dogs' snouts.

Cat owners could be particularly humorous and inventive. If a cat owner did not have a carrier, they made one themselves. This is where imaginations and resourcefulness came in. I saw cats brought into the exam room in pillow cases, shirts, coats, waste baskets, paper bags, clothes hampers, baby carriages, plain cardboard boxes, suitcases, and under blouses. There was a segment of my clientele that was industrious as well as creative. They built their own cat carriers out of plywood and hardware cloth. Some were so big and heavy that a grown man was needed to carry them in. The doors and latches varied. Some had brass hinges, a doorknob, and a bolt. Other doors had wire for hinges and a nail, stick, or a tie from a loaf of bread to secure the door. I should have taken pictures of all the different kinds of homemade carriers that I saw. It would have made a great coffee table book.

One client used to come into the clinic with his cat on his shoulder.

No matter what was happening in the waiting room, that cat would simply sit on the shoulder as if nothing was happening. In the exam room when I talked to the client, the cat was eye level, staring at me as if he was part of the conversation. They even came to my rabies clinics at the fire station that way, and believe me, rabies clinics are a zoo with dogs barking and lunging at cats or other dogs. But this cat never made a move. I actually examined and gave vaccinations with him on the owner's shoulder. I've never seen anything like that again.

Sometimes the humans in the clinic were the ones who provided the levity. One Sunday morning I went to the vet hospital to treat a patient, and I found the kennel girl cleaning kennels. This young lady eventually became a vet and actually practiced in nearby Bangor. When I greeted her she seemed very nervous—no eye contact, short, quick answers, not focused on her chores. For some reason I needed to go down to the basement to get something, and when I got to the bottom of the stairs I came face to face with a tall, blond young man. I jumped back and he just stood there, stiff as a board, staring at me like a deer in the headlights. Once I regained my composure and realized I was not in danger, I found out he was my kennel person's boyfriend. I imagine my kennel girl was having a canary at that moment. What were the chances I would go down the basement? Having friends in the hospital was not allowed. As calmly as I could, I asked him to leave. As calmly as he could, he did. I came back upstairs and finished my treatments, never saying a word. I didn't have to.

During one office call my tech, Fran, was helping me with a dog on the exam table. She was holding the head, I was examining the rear, and the owner was standing between us. I started to explain what I was seeing to the owner. I turned to her, but she was gone. Fran and I looked at each other in shock. Where did she go? We then looked down at the floor. She had gone into a dead faint and had quietly folded to the floor between us.

Of course, sometimes I was the one who would inadvertently add to the fun. I was once about to examine an old poodle on the exam table. The owner was holding the dog, and her grown daughter was standing in back of us, trying not to get in the way. Back then I had 5x7 cards that had both the pet's and the owner's names on top. I quickly looked at the poodle's card to check for the dog's name. As I approached the poodle, I said in a cutesy high-toned voice, "How is our little Mitzi doing today?" From behind me I heard, "I'm fine, Doc." Mitzi was the daughter's name; Pearl was the dog's name—I'd misread the file! To be fair, their names were close together on the file and Mitzi does sound like a dog's name. I didn't move; I was catatonic for a second. I kept my eyes fixed on the dog, not wanting to make eye contact with the mom. All I could muster was, "Oh, that's good," and then I took out my stethoscope and proceeded to pretend to listen to Pearl's very healthy sounding, normal heart.

Surgery was fun. I spent two mornings a week performing spays, neuters, lump removals and other procedures. During surgery, my anesthetic tech, Deb, would assist me in inducing and prepping the patient, and then she would monitor anesthesia during surgery. We would chit chat or listen to the radio. When we listened to music, I asked Deb to turn down the volume when Journey, Foghat, or REO Speedwagon came on. I didn't like their songs. After a while it became a joke, and she would turn up the volume just to tease me. I was powerless to turn the radio down, as my hands were usually indisposed. All I could do was laugh. Other times we listened to the psychologist Dr Laura. Over the years Deb and I would try to guess what Dr Laura was going to recommend after hearing the person's predicament. We got pretty good at it. We imagined hanging our counseling shingle out and taking our own clients. Deb was also very tolerant of my swearing when a surgery went sideways. A few of my techs didn't like helping in surgery because of my expletives. Deb, on the other hand, didn't care. She knew it was a way for me to vent frustration. She never let on, but I think she could have taught me a few new ones.

The clinic atmosphere could turn on a dime. Emergencies like car accidents, seizures, or bleeding wounds would drop in unannounced, and humor needed to take a back seat pretty quickly, so we tried to stay positive and see things in a funny way whenever we could. Humor is a good medicine for stress.

*  *  *  *

Afterthoughts by Dr Jefferson:

John, I don't think you ever had to look for humor. It's just part of who you are. You had me laughing within 10 minutes of meeting you at our teacher orientation class at York Community College.

I'd like to hear more about the basement encounter with your kennel girl's boyfriend. That Sunday, when she saw you drive in, I imagine she said, "Quick, go hide in the basement, he never goes down there." What ever happened after that? Did you scare him so bad that you killed a budding romance?

I'd also like to comment on dogs and donuts. Why so surprised? Look at what you feed them. Dried kibbles? You really can't blame him for taking advantage of accessible donuts.

## Dr Jefferson: The Wedding Ring

Bonnie and I were married on June 12, 1965. I told myself I would never take the wedding band off my 3rd finger, left hand. Actually, I didn't take it off, it ... but that's my story.

It happened at my first job out of veterinary school. As a general practice we saw everything from one-ounce gerbils to one-ton draft horses. I accepted the job offer because the practice emphasis was dairy cows. At the time that's where my heart was. I would see an occasional dog or cat back at the office, but I much preferred working in cow and horse barns.

Cows have a nine-month gestation and are bred to produce a calf about the same time each year. Most cattle births are unattended and things work out fine. Occasionally a cow at term will push and look like she's going to give birth, but doesn't. That situation has to be checked out. It usually means that the calf is in an incorrect position, which will block a normal delivery. Normal presentation is front feet first with the soles down. Then the nose appears with the calf's head resting on top of those front legs. Sometimes the legs will poke out, but no head appears. This means that the head is turned back to the left or right or sometimes down between the front legs.

Another awkward presentation is a breech birth. In that case the first thing you see is the tail. A breeched calf is really stuck, and getting it unstuck is a major project. It isn't as easy as 'just turn them around," as there is no room in the pelvis to do that. Sometimes twins will complicate things by both trying to arrive at the same time. Some farmers are adept at straightening out calves that are hung up. Usually, however, they have to call for a large animal vet. Part of our training in vet school is learning how to manipulate a fetus so the birth can proceed. Rarely, the calf is just too big to fit through the canal, and a Caesarian may be indicated.

I had been with the practice several months and was enjoying everything about the job. I was headed home one midafternoon when I got a call on the Motorola radio in my vehicle—again, long before cell phones. The receptionist at the office was reporting a difficult birth in a cow at Bob Johnson's place. I was there within 20 minutes. Bob was milking, and as I entered the barn, he said, "It's Belle, Doc. She's over in the calf barn. She's been trying since noon, and nothing is showing. I'd help you out, but I'm right in the middle of milking."

"No problem, I'll go check her out."

I stopped in the milk room to fill my stainless steel pail with warm water and made my way to the calf barn. That barn had two calving stalls, each 12 by 12 feet. Belle, the big Holstein in trouble, was lying on her side in one of the stalls on a deep bed of straw. She would push, pick her head up, look toward her tail, flop her head down and breathe hard for a few minutes. Bob was right, nothing was showing, and it didn't look like she was making progress. I found a halter, put it on her head, and tied her loosely to one of the steel pipes that formed her stall.

"OK, darling, looks like you're having a hard time. Let's take a look."

Getting ready for a bovine internal exam involves a number of steps taken in a certain order. The first thing is to get and keep the tail out of the way. Baling twine is tied to the switch on the end of the cow's tail. The other end is tied around one of her front legs. Then the whole back end of the cow is washed with a soapy disinfectant in a water solution using wads of cotton. Next, the examiner's arm is scrubbed from hand to shoulder. After that, a long sterile disposable plastic sleeve with a glove at the end is pulled on. The shoulder end is attached to your shirt with a clip, and a sterile lubricant is liberally applied to the entire sleeve. Now you are ready. The finger tips are pressed together making the hand into a cone shape, and you gently insert it into the birth canal. Cows generally tolerate this exam without a fuss.

Because Belle was lying flat out on her side I had to crouch down behind her. I inserted my right hand and immediately ran into the calf's nose. The calf's head filled the entire birth canal. That left me no room to get to the legs that were still folded up within the uterus instead of presenting with the head. I knew that I needed to use both hands to get everything straightened out. I stood up and went through the same procedure of scrubbing and putting a sterile sleeve on my left arm. Then, because I had broken sterility, I put a new sterile sleeve over the right arm.

Now I had to get myself down into a prone position. That was awkward because I couldn't touch anything with my hands or arms, or I would void the sterility. Essentially I squatted and then dropped down onto my butt. My arms were out straight so I wouldn't touch anything. I rolled so that I was on my side, keeping my arms and hands off the bedding.

With my left hand, I pushed the head back in as much as I could. I had to wait out the times that Bella was pushing against me. I pushed and held, pushed and held. With the head back in a bit I had just enough space to get my right arm by it to reach way in and find a leg. I walked my fingers down to the foot. Cupping it in my hand, I pulled it up from the uterus into the birth canal. After ten minutes of this, the sleeve on my left arm became detached from the clip at my shoulder and slid down my wrist. Now it was in the way. I was getting concerned because the cow was pushing harder. She wanted that calf out of there! It was getting to be a crisis, and there was no more time for niceties. I yanked both sleeves off, slathered more lubricant onto my bare arms, and dove back in. There! I found the other foot and guided it up into the canal. Now a few heroic pushes by Belle, and the calf was delivered. I was just as happy as Belle. Both of us lay there for a minute, exhausted. The calf started breathing right away and was soon on her feet. I left them to bond and went back to the milk room to wash up. As I soaped up my left hand, I realized that something was missing—my wedding ring! The combination of the gooey lubricant, the amniotic fluid, and all my twisting and pulling had caused it to slip off my finger.

I returned to the calf barn and moved Belle to the other stall. Her new baby followed along. Returning to the maternity stall I took a pitchfork and shook all the straw out, hoping I would hear a ping as the ring hit the floor. No luck. I returned to Belle and tied her where she could get at her hay. The calf began to nurse, and Belle passed the afterbirth. I sifted through that placenta, but there was no ring there. I went through the scrubbing and gloving procedure again on my right arm, and then slid back into the birth canal and down into the now rapidly contracting uterus. I carefully swept the folds of the uterus. As far as I could tell, there was no ring.

I cleaned up and checked in with Bob who was just getting his milking done.

*Dog and Pony Show*

"Bob, you've got a cute heifer, and everyone is OK. The calf decided to not come out for a while, but we worked it out." I told him about the ring and the possibility of it acting as an IUD. I explained that it might prevent a future pregnancy. He said he would keep an eye out for the ring, but it never surfaced.

I kept track of Belle. She had a calf every year. Each was an easy delivery. She lived a long life. If this happened today, I'd be able to find the ring in Belle with an ultrasound machine. We didn't have those back then. I've thought since that a metal detector would have found it in the stall. Bonnie bought me a new wedding band for our next anniversary. I lost that one too, but that's another story.

When reproductive ultrasounds first became available to veterinarians, I was excited! That incredible diagnostic machine gave me the ability to diagnose an equine pregnancy just 15 days after breeding. A week later and I was able to see if the mare was carrying twins. By day 28 the heartbeat is visible, which was always a thrill.

My favorite client in those days was Nancy. She asked me to ultrasound a Standardbred mare at her farm in Cornish. In the past this particular mare had always been tough to get in foal, and her pattern had settled down to foaling every other year rather than annually. Last year's foal by her side was now a promising yearling. Nancy wanted another from her mare next year. In mid-March, 15 days after she was bred, I ultrasounded the mare and told Nancy there was no visible embryo. I did note two medium-sized cysts in the uterine wall, which are fairly common and of no real concern. My advice to Nancy was to breed her again when she came back into heat. She didn't show another heat, so Nancy had me come back in two weeks to see why. This second ultrasound at 30 days agreed with the first. She was not in foal. She never did come back into heat that spring, so Nancy decided to wait until the next year, which was normal for her anyway.

Nancy was a vet's dream client. She knew all the animals on her farm really well: her dog, two cats, and all ten horses. When Nancy said something wasn't right, something wasn't right. In the late fall she thought the mare was getting kind of chubby, but didn't think too much of it. She decreased her grain ration a little. Toward the end of October she called to say that she thought the mare was pregnant. I said,

"No, Nancy, can't be. That second ultrasound was a full month after her breeding, and if she were pregnant, we would have seen it on the screen."

Nancy replied, "Wanna bet?"

"Sure," I said. "How about this? I'll come out and do a rectal exam and if she's pregnant, you don't owe me a thing. If she's not, you will owe me the usual charges."

"Done!" said Nancy, and because she sounded so sure of herself, I began to doubt myself. Nancy's farm is an hour away, so I timed the visit for the next time I was in her town. That way, if I was wrong, I wouldn't be out as much gas money.

Nancy brought her mare out of the stall and onto the floor of the barn. Nancy was right, she did look pretty chunky. Mmmmm. I counted on my fingers. This would be over seven months since her breeding. If she was pregnant, she would be foaling in four months. I pulled on a rectal sleeve and slathered my arm with lubricant. No need to take the ultrasound probe in with me. At seven months I could almost shake hands with the fetus, which by then would be the size of a cocker spaniel. I squeezed the fingers of my hand into a cone shape and pushed my hand and then my arm into her rectum. I pushed a little further so my arm was in, just past my elbow. At this stage of pregnancy (if she was) right under my hand there would be what felt like a big water-filled balloon, the uterus. If you keep your hand flat and gently bounce the uterus, the head, trunk, or legs of the foal will float up against your hand. There is also usually a reflex pulling away by the foal. All that happened. I was happy for Nancy, but embarrassed for me.

"Nancy, looks like you just got yourself a free farm call. She is definitely pregnant, and the foal is alive and kicking. You can expect a baby in mid-February." Nancy was overjoyed. I had some explaining to do. In thinking about it. I suspect the embryo was behind one of the cysts and so not visible when I ultrasounded the mare.

On February 20, Nancy called and told me to come out and check the new baby. I asked, "Colt or filly."

She said, "I have a surprise for you when you come out, and you'll see then." I arrived at her farm that afternoon and saw a stud colt nursing his mom. I gave the colt an exam and announced that he was perfect.

"So Nancy, what's the surprise? "

"Oh, I thought you'd be interested in his name."

"Sure, what are you calling him? "

Nancy said, "If the association approves, his name is 'Jefferson's Mistake!' "

"Oops, guess I had that coming. Can I tell you, I hope he makes it as a race horse? If he does, I'll make it a point not to be there any time he's racing. I wouldn't be able to stand all the harassment I'd get."

Although he looked promising, he was one of those horses that just didn't care if he won a race or not, so he never won, placed, or even showed. However, he did race and his name, or rather our name, was in the racing programs for a season. Finally Nancy decided he wasn't competitive and decided not to race him. He was eventually sold to someone as a riding horse. Thankfully the new owners changed his name.

\* \* \* \*

Afterthoughts by Dr Hunt:

Wait a minute, Dave—you lost two wedding rings? The first story is a pretty tall tale—did Bonnie believe you? I think you owe it to our readers to narrate the second lost ring story; I bet it's a humdinger!

I stayed at a bed and breakfast in Canada shortly after graduating from vet school. When the proprietor found out I was a vet, he told me that he had a cow ready to give birth and he would come get me if there were any problems. I wasn't sure if he was kidding. I helped with a few calvings in school, but never on my own. I didn't sleep all night, scared to death I would be awakened to go out to the barn. At breakfast the owner smiled at me and said the cow had birthed a beautiful little girl and that their vet had come to help. I dodged that large-animal bullet. Dave makes it look easy. It's not.

One Christmas Eve a client came in with her rather large-bellied black Lab. She wanted to know if the dog was pregnant. She did not want puppies on Christmas morning, and I didn't blame her. The dog looked pregnant to me but was too large to feel the puppies. I took an x-ray that came out very grainy. In those days we didn't have a digital x-ray developer; we were at the mercy of developer tanks. I couldn't see puppies on the x-ray, but I told her that I couldn't say one way or another if the dog was pregnant. The owner threatened to call me on Christmas morning to take care of the puppies. I couldn't tell if she was kidding. Well, I got a call the day after Christmas telling me the bitch had given birth to ten healthy puppies, and the owner didn't sound happy. In a small town, mistakes like that don't go unnoticed, nor are they soon forgotten. Eventually the owner forgave me and small town life went on. Over the years I would be reminded of my diagnostic blunder, but with a smile.

# Chapter 13
Memorable Clients

# Dr Hunt: Clients, the Other Half of Vet Medicine

Veterinary medicine is just as people-oriented as it is animal-centered. At times, caring for animals was the easy part—it was dealing with the pet owners that was challenging. I saw clients at their best, like when they brought in a new kitten, and at their worst, like when they brought in their dog that was in a house fire.

I was a "people vet;" I cared for my clients' wellbeing as much as the pets'. They went hand in hand. Without a good working relationship with a client, I could not adequately provide care for the pet. When a client was my partner I was able to provide the best medicine within the constraints of the client's capabilities (financial, home care, transportation, emotional strength). Dealing with people is a mixture of intuition and learning. Some vets don't have an intuitive personality, while some never learn from their mistakes. I worked with a vet at a five-man practice in Connecticut. He loved doing surgery, and was good at it, but he had no use for people and didn't care to change. He never showed empathy or concern towards his clients, and he didn't care if he lost a client. He could get away with that nonsense because the practice was large enough to lose a client and go unnoticed. That behavior would never fly in a small town like Bucksport.

When I entered an exam room, I had to do two things simultaneously: look at my patient, and greet and assess my client. I needed to profile the pet owner, even if I knew them, to determine their frame of mind, including the motive for bringing in their pet. Knowing the pet owner's demeanor directed me as to how I was going to examine the patient and discuss treatment options.

I wasn't always right in sizing up clients. One time, my profile of a client was so off base I almost lost a client and friend. It started out as an emergency call on a Sunday night. The message on my beeper was something like, "My cat is really sick; call me immediately." I didn't recognize the name showing up on my beeper. The neighboring vet and I alternated calls, so he could have been one of his clients. I dialed the number and identified myself when he answered. "It's about time," he said.

"What's the problem?" I asked.

"You tell me," he said. That put me on guard and in a bad mood. I kept my cool and asked him what the cat was doing that worried him. He replied that it was crying in pain and I needed to see him—NOW! After some more questioning (and snippy answers), he finally told me the cat was squatting in the litter box while crying in pain and had been doing so all day. I wanted to say, "Why didn't you call me earlier in the day?" That was enough information to warrant immediate emergency action. The cat was blocked. He couldn't urinate and kidney failure and death was possible. I said to come right down. He simply hung up. I assumed that meant he was coming. I lived only a few minutes from my clinic, so I waited nervously for his arrival. I had no records on any of his pets and was hoping I would never see him again after this visit.

When he arrived, I saw a man in his 50s of solid build, medium height and, of all things, a flat-top crew cut. That style was big in the early sixties, but now you only see that type of hair style in the military. He came in, no smile, but I could see he was worried. I wasn't going to be bullied and told what to do, yet as a veterinarian my duty was to help animals regardless of the owner. So, I put forth my professional face with my mark of sympathy. I kept my humorous part of me to myself. He grumbled hello and mumbled something about how he heard I was new here. I assessed the situation and told him the cat needed to be hospitalized. I had to unblock him that night, and he should call in the morning. He looked surprised, and I could see his square jaw and keen eyes soften just a tad. I worked on his cat into the early morning hours. The next morning I called him to report that the cat was doing fine, and after a few days he would be able to go home. Silence on the other end of the phone. My knuckles were white gripping the phone. Holy cow, did I screw up and mishandle this guy. Finally he said, in a softened voice, "Thank you, Dr Hunt." I almost fainted.

When he picked up his cat, he was a different man. He initially appeared as a gruff general, but from that time onward he was the friendliest, most respectful, sweetest guy I came to know in Bucksport. For years, every time he came to the clinic he gave everyone Hershey

Kisses. Whenever I found two Hershey Kisses on my desk, I knew he had dropped by for some cat food. During one visit he gave everyone a $2 bill. To this day I still have his $2 bill in my wallet. When he passed away a few years back, I showed it to his wife during an office visit and we both wept in the privacy of the exam room. I learned first impressions need to be treated very carefully.

You just don't know where people are coming from when they come to the vet clinic. People bring their emotional and personal baggage in with them. I guess people feel veterinary offices are safe places for them to vent, lash out, or reveal private things. For instance, Steve was a Dr Jekyll/Mr. Hyde client. He would storm into the reception area and rudely make demands on my staff. When he came into the exam room with his German Shepherd, he turned into a polite and respectful guy. I had breakfast with him a number of times and even after getting to know him I still couldn't figure out why he acted so badly towards my staff. His girlfriend, who was as sweet as can be, saw what was happening but seemed powerless to correct his bad behavior. When my staff told me he made them cry due to his rudeness, I decided he crossed the line. No one does that to my staff, and I told him so. He was better after that.

Some clients weren't aggressive or abrasive in their behavior, but still found a way to make their presence known. Occasionally, when I was doing surgery in the back of the clinic I would hear this very loud voice coming from the reception area. I knew it was a member of what I called the Loud Family. The entire family yelled when they talked, and their dogs were loud barkers too! I swear I needed ear plugs when I was in the exam room with them. After they left, I had to consciously scale back my voice for the next client because I ended up yelling right along with the Loud Family during their office visit.

On the flip side, I had the most wonderful, caring, friendly clients anyone could wish for. One emergency call late one night I had to bring my three young children with me because I didn't want to leave them alone at the house. The emergency was an injured dog brought in by a couple that I had known for years. The husband helped me bring the dog into the surgery room and actually assisted me in treating his dog, and his wife stayed in my car with my three children as a babysitter.

Most of my clients were easy to work with. I respected their circumstances and how they felt about their pets, and I always worked with them to provide the best care I could. Clients showed their appreciation with tasty goodies. I had a fisherman from Stonington drop off the best crab meat I've ever tasted. Another client was a mussel farmer, and he would drop off a bag of mussels every so often. Christmas time meant our break room was full of homemade goodies my staff eagerly waited for each year. Many of my office calls turned into chat sessions. I would get updates on family news or town gossip. There were certain clients my staff knew to book two appointments for, knowing the visit would be half vet care, half socializing.

My clinic reflected my personality, values, and a level of care I would give my own pets.

*  *  *  *

Afterthoughts by Dr Jefferson:

Vet clients are often emotional about their animal's condition when they come to us. In addition, being human, they are always carrying their own problems with them. John and I both learned to make allowances for things said. Even so, if you want to get any medical professional annoyed, don't be a wise guy like John's client who, when asked what the problem was, answered "You tell me." We've heard it before, but our gut reaction is to show that client the door.

# Dr Jefferson: Best Friend Forever

Private practice in veterinary medicine is a business, but you do make some wonderful friends. This is how my client, Darcie, saved the day for me 20 years ago and became my BFF. Darcie was in her mid-20s at the time. She was a hard worker with a small stable of racing Standardbreds. Darcie not only trained her string of horses, she drove them in races. I believe her animals appreciated her kindness. She seemed to trust me, and it was a pleasure to work for her.

I had just examined a Standardbred gelding for Darcie at the Cumberland Race Track. When I was done, I jumped into my vehicle and went tearing out of the fairgrounds, already late for my next appointment 10 miles away. I drove at 50, right past the very visible 40 mph speed limit sign. I was crowding 55 when I saw the blue lights in my mirror. I had three quick thoughts.

Number 1: Where was *he* hiding?

Number 2: Now I'm *really* going to be late!

And Number 3: This is going to cost me at least *$100!*

I pulled over, and one of Cumberland's finest pulled in behind me. I reached toward the glove box for the registration, muttering under my breath. I had just grabbed the paperwork when I was startled by a horn blaring behind me. I looked over my left shoulder to see Darcie's truck go roaring past the cop as he was getting out of his cruiser. She pulled up in front of me, skidding on the dirt shoulder as she hit the brakes. She jumped out with her motor still running and door left wide open like a bird with an injured wing. There I sat with a town cop walking toward me from behind, carrying his ticket book, and Darcie running toward me from in front. They arrived at my window at the same time. The officer looked confused, which is exactly how I felt. Before he had a chance to open his mouth, Darcie shouted, "Doc, ya gotta get back to the track! That gelding you were working on went down, and now he's acting real crazy like he's having a fit or something. I'm afraid he's going to hurt himself. "

The officer said to me, "Are you a vet?"

"I am. I just left the racetrack, and it looks like I better get back. Can we put off our business a bit until I see what's going on with her horse?"

"Of course," he said. "Let's do a 180. I'll give you an escort back to the track." All three of us roared back to the track. It was the cop, me, and then Darcie. The blue lights were flashing and the siren wailing. I stayed close to him, both of us doing 70. Darcie followed, right on my tail.

When we got to the track entrance, the cop pulled over, rolled his window down and put his arm out to stop me. I stopped next to him and pushed the power button to open my passenger side window. He hollered out, "You go help her out, Doc. Forget that I stopped you. I hope her horse makes it. Have a good day!"

"Thanks," I shouted back. Darcie swung around both our vehicles and I followed her to the barn. All this time I had been wondering what could have made her horse go down. All I had done ten minutes before was check his legs and declared him fit to race the next day. No medication had been given.

We both pulled up to the barn, and Darcie got out with a huge grin plastered on her face. "Well, Doc, guess you owe me one."

"You mean your horse is OK, and you just ...."

"Yeah", she laughed. "I left the barn right after you and watched you take off in a dust cloud. As soon as I hit the town road, I saw the cop pull out from where he was hiding next to the mom and pop store. I figured you could use some help, so I made up the story about my horse going down to maybe save you a ticket."

My client Darcie suddenly had become my BFF! I gave her a big hug. We laughed about it for years. Whenever I left her barn, she would grin and say, "You be sure to drive slow, now. " I've wondered since whether the cop may have come from a horse background.

*Dog and Pony Show*

\* \* \* \*

Afterthoughts by Dr Hunt:

I thoroughly enjoyed that story; you can't make that stuff up. There are some pretty special people in this world, and as veterinarians we come across a few that enrich our lives. Darcie was one of them.

When I first got to Bucksport, I had a dog pass away from an unforeseen anesthetic reaction, and I was blamed for the death. The distraught owner spread the news all over town that I killed his dog. Rumors sprang up that I was even killing horses. Clients seemed scared to leave their pets for surgery. It was a pretty bleak time. But I had one client that called me up at home one night and said she had faith in me, didn't believe all that rubbish, and knew I was good at what I did. That one phone call gave me the strength to ride the rumor storm. That client never wavered from her loyalty to me. She was my Darcie.

Footnote: she was the only person I ever allowed to call me "Johnny."

# Chapter 14
## Kids

# Dr Hunt: Career Day

Young people are drawn to veterinarians because of our connection to animals. Most youngsters love animals, so who better to observe and emulate than a veterinarian? Over the years I had high schoolers request to spend a day with me to satisfy the high school's requirement for a career observation. I didn't want a teen spend a day observing office calls because they're boring, and the student would feel uncomfortable standing in the corner, so I had the would-be vets come in for a morning during my surgery day. That way I could talk to them about their interests, explain the profession, and they could observe what I thought was really neat stuff in surgery.

My surgery suite was small—large enough for a table, anesthetic machine, sink, and counter, but barely enough room to move around the table. There was a large surgery light overhead that produced a very bright light and threw out a lot of heat. It was pretty cozy for me, but not so for some of my observers. There they were, excited and nervous, standing in this warm, small room with a mask over their face, watching me cutting open an animal and trying to make conversation with the vet. I even added fuel to this proverbial fire by pointing out parts of the innards of the animal and not clamping off a small bleeder right away. I know, I'm bad.

I could tell which students would be good vets by the way they handled the observation. Their bearing, attention to detail, and careful questions hinted at strong future veterinarians. Some didn't fare so well, though—especially one young lady named Carly. She stood near the table in the warm room, the bright light shining down on the spay surgery. At the time I didn't know she hadn't had any breakfast. I was gabbing away, pointing out the ovaries and uterus as I took them out of the dog's abdomen. At first, she was asking questions, but then I noticed she was quiet. I looked up and I saw Carly's eyes were not focused, and she looked pale even behind the mask. Then she started to sway like a tree on a windy day. The gentle swaying turned into a full-blown rocking, and down she went in a dead faint. As Carly fell, she hit her head on the drywall. I couldn't help her, I was right in the middle of tying off the uterus, so my surgery tech helped her off the floor and had her sit on a stool in the treatment area. As I was finishing the surgery, I noticed a perfectly round dent in the drywall near the floor. Later, I talked to Carly and evaluated her for a concussion (something I had to learn to do as a high school coach). Besides a small bump, only her pride was hurt. My initial intention was to repair the drywall dent, but as time went on, I decided to keep Carly's head imprint and use it as an example for future observers. From then on, my technicians instructed observers to have breakfast before coming to surgery. When future vets were standing in surgery, I would ask, "Did you have breakfast this morning?" Before they answered, I said, "See that round dent in the drywall? That was from my last observer who fainted because she didn't have breakfast!" My mask hid my Cheshire cat smile. Nine times out of ten I sent the potential future partner to our break room to grab one of the pastries we had for coffee breaks.

The dent was still there when I sold my practice. I pointed it out to the new owner, who loved the story. I wonder if the new vet points it out to her observers.

*  *  *  *

Afterthoughts by Dr Jefferson:

It's interesting how your first surgery can affect you. John's surgery room even has the scars to prove it. I have had a number of adults, mostly grown men, who took a nose dive during a horse castration. I learned to glance at their face and look for the telltale sweat on their forehead. If I asked, "Are you OK?" they often would say, "I'm fine, blood don't bother me." Then when I crunched the spermatic cord—over they'd go. All my castrations were done in a field, so I never worried about concussions as they always went down on soft grass. I kept doing my job, and they usually recovered and were standing before the horse did, always very embarrassed. Funny how males have to make excuses: "I didn't eat breakfast," just like Carley in John's story. I never understood that excuse. It was the blood, silly, not your lack of food this morning. Taking a dive doesn't make you less of a man.

# Dr Jefferson: Life Lesson

Because of my profession, when the kids in our neighborhood had a living thing question, I was the go-to guy. One spring morning I was out sweeping the driveway. I looked over at the empty lot next door and saw a group of four youngsters. My son Jim was the oldest, at six. My daughter Tally and the other two kids were between four and five. They were all down on their knees huddled over something. I thought, *Wonder what they've got there?* I heard one of them say, "Let's ask him." They rose as one, with Jim in the center, holding something very carefully in his hands. The rest of the kids were grouped around him as they slowly walked toward me, all concentrating on their find. Their eyes were shiny with excitement.

"Look what we found," Tally said. "Can you fix him? Can we keep him?" There, cradled in Jim's hands was a small sparrow. It was feathered and probably just two or three weeks old. It reflexively opened and closed its little beak. I thought, *It won't last the day.*

"Wow, where did you find him? " I asked.

"Right out here in the field. He was just lying there. We're afraid a cat will get him. He can't fly."

"You're right. He's way too young to fly. Do you think he fell from a nest?" We looked over at the treeless, empty lot.

"Maybe," I ventured, "he did fall out of his nest. It could be that a cat found him under a tree and carried him in his mouth to the field." Our neighborhood had a healthy cat population.

"But, why did the cat leave him here?"

"Great question. Cats like to play with birds they've caught. Maybe this little guy was too hurt to react, and the cat just left him." I anticipated the next question, which wasn't long in coming. "We could find some worms and feed him. Would that be OK?"

I took the bird from Jim and held him in my left hand. I pinched his little feet and got no response. I knew what had to be done.

"Well, that would be a nice thing to do, but who's going to teach him to fly?" Now my mind was racing. "Kids, I think he is dying and that we should get ready to bury him. Run home and find me a little box and something soft we can put around him." Debbie and her brother David ran home. Jim went into our garage, brought out our shovel, walked into the field, and started digging.

Everyone came back quickly. We walked toward Jim who had a hole about a foot deep. I held the bird tightly with the fingers of my hand. As I walked, I made a quick motion with my thumb to break the bird's neck. OH NO! To my shock his head came off. I had pushed too hard. I used my index finger and thumb to put his head back on his shoulders. Here I am, a former US Marine, panicked over what these kids are going to think of me. I looked at them carefully. No one had seen or suspected that I had just decapitated the bird.

We stood over the hole Jim had dug. I brought the sparrow closer to my face, looked at him carefully, and said, "It looks like he has stopped breathing. It was great that you were all here to find him, I'm sure he felt your love. Now, I'll hold onto him, and if you want you can pat him gently to say goodbye." The bird was lying in the palm of my hand, and my fingers were around his body. With my thumb I kept a little pressure on the top of his head to keep everything connected. Each of the kids took a turn to gently say goodbye. It had become a solemn occasion.

Debbie had found a small shoe box at home, and David brought a dish towel. I took the towel and wrapped the bird in it and placed him in the box. I was careful to tuck a bunch of the towel tightly next to the bird's neck so there would be no danger of things coming apart. Jim put the cover on the shoe box and placed it in the hole. I took a handful of dirt and said, "Here's another way of saying goodbye." I threw it onto the box. Each of the kids did the same. Jim filled the hole with the shovel and patted the dirt level. David found a stone and he placed it on top of the little grave.

Last night I called my daughter, Tally, now in her 50s, to see if she remembered the incident.

"Oh, of course, it was one of the standout memories of my childhood." I asked her why. She said "You were my hero. I completely accepted that you knew all about life and death. If you said the bird wasn't going to live, that was how it was." I told her that it was probably time she heard the rest of the story and fessed up about how the bird lost his head that day. Time had done its healing, and we had a good laugh about it. Life, trauma, and death. Another day in the neighborhood.

I was always conscious of clients' kids in the barns I visited. I never thought of them as being underfoot and tried to involve them in what I was doing if possible. If I was examining a horse and could see one hanging around, I asked, "Would you like to hear your horse's heartbeat?" I put the bell over the horse's heart and set the ear pieces into little ears. The expressions on their faces as they heard the slow boom-boom were always fun to see. Occasionally parents would try to send their children up to the house if we were doing a surgery such as a castration. I would always argue for them staying and watching. I felt like it was a great learning opportunity. Families that have animals are one step ahead in child rearing as their kids experience birth, sickness, and death with their pets.

*  *  *  *

Afterthoughts by Dr Hunt:

Dave's bird story reminded me of the James Harriot story about when an elderly client's parakeet died in his hand. He excused himself, not telling the owner what happened, got a replacement from a lady in town, and returned to the client, who never realized it was a different parakeet.

Dave managed to hold onto the head, the kids never suspecting, and he taught his kids how to accept death and respect all animals that pass. Clients frequently asked me what they should tell their kids when the family cat or dog had to be put to sleep. I always answered, "the truth." I once had a youngster raise his hand during one of my vet talks at the local elementary school and yell out, "My dad said you killed my dog." Why a parent would tell a child that is mystifying. The pet may have died during my care due to illness, or perhaps I put them to sleep, but I never killed a pet in my life. This parent either didn't have the courage to face the truth or he was very angry at losing his pet so he had to blame somebody. Either way, the parent wasn't helping his child like Dave helped his.

# Chapter 15
EMERGENCY!

## Dr Hunt: The Dreaded Late Night Phone Call

If you read the fine print on the job description, you will discover that vets have to attend to emergency situations no matter what day or time. Christmas day, Saturday night, Sunday morning, birthdays—it doesn't matter, animals don't pick and choose when they need lifesaving care.

For years, I was on emergency call for fifty per cent of my evenings and days off. I shared this dubious chore with a vet in the town next to me. When I got home from a long day with the emergency beeper in tow, I could never really relax. I went through the motions of an evening—eating dinner, bathing the kids, putting them to bed, and maybe listening to TV, but all the while I knew that beeper would go off, typically after I went to bed. When I heard the beeper in the middle of the night, it startled me at first, and then I always swore.

Clients were rarely in a calm, coherent mood when I called them back. Trying to figure out if there was an emergency was the first hurdle. Half the time there was not. Sometimes the person on the phone acted as a relay, trying to get information from someone in another room of the house. That was fun. I would ask a question, then the person on the phone would yell (into the phone) to someone who was somewhere in another part of the house, who would then give an irritated or angry muffled response. I would eventually get a partial answer from the person on the phone, but only after a frustratingly long conversation. It was like playing the telephone game with five year olds.

Vets need to learn a specific skill set in deciphering what a client is saying when they are in crisis mode. They don't teach that in vet school. I frequently had people yelling on the phone, "My cat is dying," or "My dog's leg bone is sticking out," or "My pet is bleeding to death." All of these could be true, but I just wasn't sure, so further questioning was required in order to find out if a bone was indeed sticking out of the dog's leg.

Once I figured out that the pet needed to be seen, I needed to make sure to inform the client that payment was needed at the time of service. I could skip this step if they were one of my regular clients, but I had been snookered more than once by clients I didn't know. After attending to a stranger's pet at midnight, the owner might say that they didn't have any money, or they forgot the check book, or they didn't have a credit card, or, my favorite, that they'd be back the next day to pay the bill. All of these excuses were bogus. Some people even copped the attitude that I should be treating their pet for free because I loved animals so much. It was hard not to become bitter, resentful, and angry at these people. Fortunately, they were a minority.

One evening I did get a call from a client I knew and really liked. George was in his 60s, short, and always dressed like an old farmer, with big baggy overalls, suspenders that were always twisted, and an old plaid shirt. His beard was salt and pepper and looked like a mouse nest, but he had kind, gentle eyes with a childlike twinkle. His 95-pound Weimaraner, Winston (by the way, Weimaraner's aren't supposed to be 95 pounds), had gotten into a discussion with a porcupine, and the porcupine won the argument. Winston was frantically trying to remove a face full of quills with his paws which resulted in the quills going in deeper and also sticking to his paws. The dog and the owner were frantic. I would jump over the moon for a client like George, and I told him on the phone to get to the vet hospital ASAP.

As they entered the front door of the hospital, I didn't see Winston at first because he was behind George, pawing at his face. George was yanking on the leash like someone trying to get an old stubborn mule to move. George and I dragged Winston into the treatment area in the back of the hospital. George was out of breath and looking a little gray, but he was going to have to be my assistant. In those days I never called my technicians in for emergencies. I did all my emergencies alone with the occasional help from the client. My clients never seemed to mind helping, and George was no exception. He was happy to help restrain Winston—who was a nice dog but had no manners—while I injected an anesthetic in his front leg. George wrapped his left arm under Winston's neck, leaned on top of Winston and grabbed his elbow with his right hand to extend the leg out to me, trying to avoid getting pricked by a quill all the while. I put a tourniquet around Winston's foreleg, grabbed

Winston's front leg, and inserted the needle attached to a large syringe full of anesthetic into the vein. Winston didn't react to the needle, but he was still frantic about the quills, so he was restless, but George was holding him steady. I had injected about half the anesthetic when George suddenly let go of Winston's leg and fell back onto the wall. He looked even paler than before and started to grip his arm and the left side of his chest, panting and trying to speak. Winston was only half anesthetized, which meant he was still excitable and actually trying to stand up to run away. I gripped the syringe as hard as I could against Winston's leg so the needle would stay in the vein. Here was the moment of truth: do I attend to George, who was apparently having a heart attack, or finish injecting the anesthetic so I wouldn't have to deal with a half crazed, 95-pound dog with a face full of quills, running around the hospital as I was calling 911. For that split second, I was paralyzed. I decided to inject the rest of the anesthesia while trying to assess George's situation. Once the dog was knocked out, I went over to George before calling an ambulance. The pain seemed to have passed and he was feeling better. He sat quietly against the wall as I pulled quills. By the time Winston was awake enough to go home, George was feeling well enough to drive, against my wishes. I had him call me when he got home. I believe he did end up having bypass surgery. For years after that emergency call, George showed his gratitude by occasionally dropping off a bag of candy at the reception desk.

You just never know what to expect from late night calls. You've got to love the job, and not just the animals, to survive veterinary medicine.

\* \* \* \*

Afterthoughts by Dr Jefferson:

In most areas small animal clinics now automatically refer their emergencies, evenings and weekends. They are referred to hospitals that just see emergencies, so this chapter will never be experienced by many vets graduating today. There is a trend now in large animal practice where a few vets in the same area establish an emergency schedule. It means that you aren't on call every night. These are welcome changes.

# Dr Jefferson: The Call from Hell

At least once a month some Mom will say to me, "It must be great being a vet. My daughter wants to do that." Or, "My son loves animals; he'd make a great vet." The attraction to animals is the first thing that steers us toward a veterinary career. There is a tendency to romanticize what animal doctors do. As an equine practitioner with 50 years in the profession, there have been wonderful moments, but there have also been times when I wished I had made a different career choice. Three years ago I journaled my thoughts at 6 a.m. after returning from one of the latter. I now refer to this particular incident as "the call from hell." Let me tell you the story.

**Mid-January, 1 a.m.:** Winter nights I go to bed early and am hard to wake up after I've been asleep for a couple of hours. When I'm on night call, I have both pager and cell phone right next to the bed, less than two feet from my head. I was in the middle of a dream, and it took me a few minutes with both noisemakers going off to realize where I was, and who I was. I threw back the covers, swung my legs over, and sat up on the edge of the bed. The pager was beeping away. It's a horrible sound. I turned it off, picked up my cell phone and pushed the green answer button. No good, they had hung up. I called the number back. Now the line is busy. Perhaps they were trying another vet. That would be good. After two more tries I got their recording and left my own.

"This is Dr J calling. Please call me back so I can help you out." I lay back down wondering if they would call and where I might be going this morning. I glanced out the window and noted the snow coming down. The outside thermometer read 22 degrees.

**Half an hour later, 1:30 a.m.:** A call from the answering service. "A Penny Watkins has called. Said you didn't answer her call. She needs a vet visit tonight. She's pretty insistent."

"OK. I have her number and I did call her but just got a recording. Did she say what's wrong?"

"No, she just said she has an emergency and says you have to come see her horse tonight."

"OK. Keep trying her number for me, and when she answers have her call my cell." The answering service lady agreed to do that. I flopped back down with phone in hand, wondering what it was, long ago, that made me think this would be a good career choice.

**15 minutes later, 1:45 a.m.:** I was staring at the ceiling, unable to sleep. My cell phone rang. I picked it up and said "Hello" as pleasantly as I could.

"Dr Jefferson? This is Penny Watkins. I've been trying to call you! My horse Johnny is in serious trouble and I need you to see him. I've tried to call you three or four times." (This wasn't true, but I'm sure she had been calling other vets and couldn't remember who she'd tried.) Penny was breathless ... the words tumbled over each other. "My horse Johnny is in terrible pain. You've got to get here right away. He's kicking the walls. He woke me out of a sound sleep, and the house is a good ways from the barn. You've got to come out. I'm afraid that he'll break his leg!"

I tried to break in. "Penny, Penny, slow down please. What do you mean he's in pain? Is he colicky? And, why is he kicking the walls?"

"No! No! I'm trying to tell you! Something is bothering his hind leg, and he woke me up kicking the stall wall. Now I'm in the barn looking at him, he's all sweaty, and his leg hurts so bad. What time can you get here? Maybe you'll have to put him down. Do you think his leg might be broken?"

The only thing I know is that horses with broken legs never kick walls. If they are still on their feet, they stand very, very still. I wasn't sure what is going on, but I knew that Penny was not happy and that I had to go see her horse.

"Penny, who is your regular vet?" She told me. It's one of the vets that I was covering for tonight, so I was obligated. "OK, what is your address so I can put it into my GPS?"

"Oh, that won't work; I'm too country here in Naples. We don't have a mailbox." I wasn't sure what that had to do with it, but I persisted.

"Penny, I need a road name and house number. I'm not setting out until I know where you live." She gave me a road name and then said that it's a private road and not a town road. I questioned her further, and she told me to look for fire lane 401. I thought, well, that's a start and wrote it down.

**2:10 a.m.:** I got dressed, had the truck running and went through my checklist: Enough gas, wallet, cell phone. GPS told me that it would take me 35 minutes to get there. Allowing for the snowy night, I guessed that it would be more like an hour. There was an inch of new snow on my driveway, and it was slippery. I dropped my Tundra into four wheel and headed out to Naples.

**35 minutes later, 2:45 a.m.:** My cell phone rang. It was Penny. "Are you on your way? I think he's worse! He's really gone wacky on me. Are you coming?"

"I'm on my way, Penny. See you in a bit."

**30 minutes later, 3:15 a.m.:** I was totally lost somewhere in the hills of Naples, Maine. Have you ever driven in a snowstorm when the wind comes from all directions? I could see maybe ten feet ahead. Beyond was a swirling whiteout bouncing my headlights back at me. Penny was right. GPS didn't get me there. I called Penny's number and was relieved to hear someone else answer the phone. I assumed it was her husband and hoped he wasn't as frantic as Penny. I told him the name of the road I just passed, and he said I was just ½ a mile away.

"Look," he said, "we're hard to find on a good day. I'll take my Explorer down to the end of our dirt road and wait for you with my flashers on." Two minutes later I spotted him and pulled over. He got out, came over to my truck, and opened my passenger front door.

"My name's Ben, I'm Penny's other half. She's the hoss crazy one, not me. Sorry you have to come out in this storm. The road up to the barn is pretty rough. Your truck looks like it can handle it. How about if I ride up with you? There's only room for one vehicle up there."

"Sure, jump in." I said. "I see you are wearing an LED headlamp. I have one just like it. Handy aren't they?"

"Yeah, I like it. You'll be glad you have it tonight."

"Why is that?"

"No power in the barn."

"Huh. Did the storm take it out?"

"Nope. I never wired the barn. I try not to do anything that might

## Dog and Pony Show

encourage this hoss business. What a waste of money! Hayburners, that's all them hosses are." I thought that this might be an interesting night. A horse lover and her husband who hates them.

Ben directed me up a rutted road that was more like a goat path. After about 100 yards we pulled up to the barn. I'm used to light pouring out of barn doors and windows when I'm at a horse emergency. This barn was darker than dark. I kept the motor running, the defroster fan on high, and stepped out into five inches of snow. I grabbed what I thought I might need from the back of the truck, settled the headlamp over my skull cap and switched it on. I noticed a light bouncing around in the barn. Must be Penny. During the hour that I spent in their barn that night, I never saw enough of Ben and Penny's faces to be able to recognize them at noon on a sunny day.

Penny was right about one thing. Her horse Johnny was not happy. Every so often he would kick back violently with his right hind leg, as if there were a crab pinching him. Penny had him crosstied, and when I looked at him and my light hit his face, he spooked and pulled back. I lowered my light so it wasn't shining in his eyes.

"Good boy. Easy now. Easy now. Gonna get you all fixed up. Whoa, whoa ... atta brave boy." I slowly reached my hand out to touch his shoulder. When I made contact he reared back, snapped the crossties, and was free. Ben and Penny went after him, their lights ricocheting off the walls in the barn. I slowly backed against a wall thinking that someone could get badly hurt here. Loose horse, in pain, scared out of his wits, and a disco light show keeping us all disoriented.

After a few minutes Ben was able to grab Johnny by the halter. Because it was so dark, I was unaware that the barn floor was soaking wet with a skim of ice on top. When I approached Ben and Johnny, both of my feet shot out in front of me like I was on ice skates. I went down like I'd been shot. I lay there on my back looking at the cobwebbed ceiling lit up by my headlamp. All my winter layers of flannel, polar fleece, and wool were instantly soaked. Two flashlight beams looked me up and down.

"How did this floor get so wet?" I asked as I slipped around trying to get upright.

Penny said, "I'm sorry, that was my fault. I was trying to soak his foot but Johnny wouldn't let me. He kept kicking the pail I had the water and Epsom salts in." Now you have to understand. Johnny really was what we call three-legged-lame. He was putting no weight on his right hind leg at all. Soaking a horse's foot is having him stand in a bucket for 20 minutes at a time. Why anyone would attempt to soak a foot when the foot is never within one foot of the floor was beyond me. I thought, for the second time tonight, about once wanting to be a vet *more than anything in the world!* I was wet, soaked through, and very, very cold.

My patient, Johnny, wanted nothing to do with me. Because all of his back weight was on his left hind, each time he kicked out with his hurting right hind, he slipped a bit on the icy floor and was thrown off balance. The horse was as frantic as Penny. I thought it would be a good idea to inject a local anesthetic near the nerves that go to the foot so he wouldn't be in so much pain. That turned out to be a bad idea. When I tried to slide a needle into his leg, he kicked fast and hard with that right hind and landed a solid shot to my thigh. I remember thinking, "It's OK, it could be worse, that *could* have been about a foot higher and then I'd be back on the floor again, except this time all curled up in a ball."

All this time Penny kept repeating over and over, "Oh, no! Oh no! He hurts so bad!" At the same time I was thinking, *Yeah, well, how about me?*

During all this, we were in total darkness except for our LED headlights flicking here and there. It looked like a Jedi light-saber battle. We quickly learned not to look directly at each other so that we wouldn't lose our night vision because of the bright lights. Crazily, that song, "Three Blind Mice" popped into my head. After five minutes of trying to inject Johnny's leg, I gave up and tried a new approach.

"Ben, have you ever used a twitch?"

"Nope, I told you I don't even like hosses."

"You're in luck tonight, Ben. Here's your chance to learn something new. Stand to the side right there and hang onto his lead. I'll put the twitch on his nose, then hand it off to you and show you how much to twist it. You want it just right, not too loose or it will come off, and not so tight that it hurts." Luckily Ben got the idea, Johnny stood very still, and I was able to get an IV tranquilizer into him. Within a minute the horse stopped fussing, and I could inject a local anesthetic just above his hoof. I told Ben to slowly unwind the twitch, and within five minutes Johnny had full weight on that right leg that had been causing him so much pain. Now maybe we could do something.

"Ben, have you ever picked up a horse's leg?"

"I told you, Doc, I don't like *hosses.*"

"Ben, I'll be straight with you. Right now it's around 4 a.m., I've never been so wet and cold, and right this minute I don't like them either. Listen, you're a rugged guy, and I really need your help. First of all, throw down some shavings or sawdust to soak up some of the water we're sloshing around in." Ben complied.

"OK, here, hand that lead to Penny, and I'll show you how to pick up and hold onto that leg." Ben was a quick learner and thankfully was rugged. He soon had the leg flexed and Johnny's lower leg resting on his thigh. I leaned around Ben and with my hoof pick started to clean out the gritty mud that was stuck to the bottom of Johnny's foot and packed hard around his frog. Right next to the frog in the deep groove called the sulcus, I hit something hard. It was a duller sound than the metallic click that says you've hit a nail. There was something big jammed deep in that space, back by the heel. It took a lot of digging from different angles to pry out whatever it was. As it hit the barn floor, all three headlamps zeroed in on it. It was an angular rock as big as the end of my thumb. Johnny probably picked it up when he was in his paddock during the day. Every time he put weight on the leg, the rock got wedged in deeper. It didn't actually penetrate the sole of the foot, but was stuck in that groove and irritating Johnny as he stepped on it. It explained why he was kicking so hard to get rid of it.

The rest was easy. I gave the horse an IV anti-inflammatory and started to gather my things. Penny told me her regular vet was due out in a few days to do spring vaccines. I didn't say it, but was relieved that it wouldn't be me. I was hoping for everyone's sake that the appointment would be during daylight hours. I took a check for my services, hoped it wouldn't bounce, and tromped through the snow on my way back to my truck.

**6:00 a.m.:** I was back home, eating an early breakfast of cold cereal before anyone else in the house was up. I was reflecting on a nearly $400 farm visit that need not have happened had Penny just kept calm and checked the bottom of her horse's foot before calling. A take home for horse owners is to make a habit of picking out the feet every time your horse is brought into the barn.

In thinking over this farm call, years later I realized that, if nothing else, my miserable incident could be made into a story, and as a writer, it's wonderful to have a story. So, to those kids who want to be vets: Do farm visits like this one that I now refer to as "the call from hell" really make me wish that I had picked a different career? At the time, yes. But in the end, stacked against all the positive things about being a vet, no way!

*****

Afterthoughts by Dr Hunt:

Before and during vet school I rode along with a large animal vet to surrounding farms. Each farm had its own unique character and obstacles when it came to vetting an animal. Dave's story shows you how large animal vets need to improvise in a moment's notice. No use bellyaching about the conditions of the farm. That won't change anything and would simply put you on the outs with your client who you may need to help out.

I had it made as a small animal vet. My patients came to my hospital, which was warm, dry, and had electricity and indoor plumbing. I have never made the claim that I loved the outdoors as much as Dave does.

# Chapter 16
## Home Remedies

# Dr Hunt: Long-Held Beliefs

Science and old wives' tales have been intertwined since time immemorial. Often, scientific facts are pushed away in favor of old remedies or fables passed on from generation to generation. Nowadays, new, often outrageous, falsehoods from the internet attempt to explain our pet's ailments or offer treatment options. I battled this war between fact and fiction my entire career. I needed to be respectful of my client's opinion while at the same time letting them know that what they thought was a good idea was actually dangerous or, at best, ineffective. I had to be careful, because some home grown treatments or old wives' tales had an element of truth in them, or had evolved from sound medical facts. Occasionally an old remedy actually had some merit, and we tried it if I thought the pet would not be harmed.

Clients often tried to treat their pet at home before calling me. I had no problem with that since I lived in a rural area where we all had to fend for ourselves at times. Consequently, old remedies used on people were tried on the pet. For instance, it was common to have people put a tea bag compress on an injured eye. Tea bags have tannic acid that tends to act as an astringent, which means it can dry out moist, swollen eye injuries. However, a tea bag can actually injure an already injured eye and make things worse, or contaminate the eye with bacteria.

Another home remedy is the use of raisins. I love this one! A client once came in with his bouncy twelve-year-old Lab. The owner stood in the middle of the exam room, feet apart, hands on hips, kind of like the Jolly Green Giant, and in a bragging tone said, "Dr. Hunt, look at my dog, doesn't he look great?" I replied, truthfully, "Why yes, he does. He looks healthy and energetic." I was wondering where this was going. I soon found out. He exclaimed, "He was stoved up (a local term to describe an animal or person unable to move or ambulate) from arthritis so I started feeding him six raisins that were soaked in gin every day. After a few weeks his arthritic pain went away and now he runs around like a puppy." How could I dispute what I was seeing in the exam room? The dog was thin and had a shiny hair coat and bright eyes. I had no option but to agree with him, and I didn't discourage him from what he was doing. Even though raisins can be harmful, six a day was under toxic levels, and the gin they were soaked in was of small consequence. Or was it? After all, my aches and pains certainly seem to go away after a few cocktails.

While doing a routine exam I sometimes discovered a round burnt circle on the dog's neck. The owner would admit he used a match (or cigarette butt) to try and remove a tick. Don't do this! A two dollar tick scoop is much safer.

Once when I opened the exam room door to check an itchy dog, I was hit with the smell of a small engine repair shop. Kerosene had been poured on the dog to treat mange. Luckily, the owner applied kerosene in spots rather than on the whole body. I don't know if kerosene actually kills mites, but it certainly can harm your pet.

People still think garlic can control worms and fleas. NO! Too much garlic can cause potentially life threatening, hemolytic anemia, although it may help ward off vampires at low doses and your pet may smell like garlic bread.

My clients frequently used hydrogen peroxide as a cleaner and antiseptic in their pet's ears. Hydrogen peroxide does an excellent job cleaning organic debris like blood, pus, and dead tissue. It does kill germs, but it is not discriminant—it harms healthy tissue too. If it is used at full strength and repeatedly in the ear it can actually do more harm than good.

Bag Balm has been a home remedy for everything, and I mean everything! Rashes, lacerations, ear infections, mouth sores, eye injuries, cysts between the toes, lumps, and even tick removal. I don't know how many times a dog came in with an injury or a skin condition that had greasy Bag Balm smeared on it. Bag Balm is a common staple in dairy barns used to help sooth chapped udders, and apparently, farmers and pet owners feel it can heal everything else too. I had issues with clients using Bag Balm to treat a hot spot. Hot spots are technically called "superficial moist dermatitis." They are wet, red, painful, hairless spots on an animal's skin secondary to excessive licking. The treatment goal is to dry them up and then treat for infection, inflammation and pain. Unfortunately, Bag Balm does not meet any of those treatment goals. Bag Balm on a hot spot actually made it harder for me to treat because the first order of business was to clip the hair around the hot spot to help dry it out. Hair that was gooey from the Bag Balm made a mess. I used to tell my clients to reserve Bag Balm for dry or chapped skin.

The ingenuity of my clients had no bounds. First aid bandaging is a prime example. A bleeding pet needs to be brought to the vet hospital, so wrapping the wound before getting into the car is paramount for obvious reasons. I saw bandage wraps that were original and at times colossal. Most people only have Band-Aids for small wounds at home, so when their pet gets a large gash, clients need to think fast. I've seen bandages made from socks, underwear, T-shirts, coats, plastic bags, saran wrap, scarves, stocking hats, and even newspapers! The bandages were wrapped with duct tape, scotch tape, masking tape, rubber bands, knee socks, scarves, shoe laces, bag ties, rope, and even wire. I often congratulated my client on his/her creativity as I tried to figure out how to unwrap this *thing* that was covering the laceration. Some laceration cases came in with a beautifully wrapped bandage that looked better than mine. The owners were usually in the medical profession. I almost hated to take it off. I should have paid them for their first aid work.

I heard this next remedy from my colleague and good friend from Blue Hill. He told me some of his clients soaked their dogs in salt water to treat any kind of skin condition or other non-descript illness. It was comforting to hear I was not the only one who heard unusual local remedies. I did recommend to my clients whose dogs tended to get allergic dermatitis from swimming in lakes that they go to the coast and swim in the ocean. The unsettled ocean has minimal pollen on its surface, thus reducing chances of allergies, and the saltwater does seem to help keep the skin healthy. However, soaking a pet in salt water seems extreme, a lot of work, and it may not help every ailment.

In addition to home remedies I heard a number of old wives' tales that ranged from reasonable to absurd. Someone once told me candy gives pets worms. When I was a kid I found a worm crawling on my Butterfingers candy bar as I pulled it out of the wrapper. Believe me, I didn't react as if I found a prize in a cereal box. Maybe someone else who fed their dog sweets had a similar experience and, voila, a new false narrative was created. Of course sweets don't give pets intestinal parasites, but they do make your dog fat.

Many people believe that a dry, warm nose on a pet always means it is sick—this isn't always true. Some dogs and cats will normally have warm, dry noses. Some pets will have noses that fluctuate from cool and moist to warm and dry during the course of a day. I wouldn't judge an animal's overall health by using its nose temperature. However, sick animals will typically have warm, dry noses, but they will also be showing other signs of illness, like: fever, lethargy, pain, etc.

Another common misconception is that a dog's lick can heal a wound. This is only partially true. When a dog licks a fresh wound it does actually aid in healing. Licking will help remove dirt and debris, which will reduce contamination and prepare the edges of the wound for healing. There is a protein in a dog's saliva that does aid in healing, but if the dog licks too much, which they invariably do, then the tongue acts like sandpaper and destroys newly forming skin, thus inhibiting first intention healing.

As a small town vet my goal was to provide the best medical care possible for my community, but I had to be flexible and open minded to treatments outside the purview of medicine. I wanted to respect the owner's idea if I could, but I didn't want it getting around that I was a quack!

*  *  *  *

Afterthoughts by Dr Jefferson:

Here's another chapter that could have been in the Funny Stories chapter. It's interesting what people swear by for treating various ailments. If we weren't already convinced of that, the Covid pandemic clinched it. I especially like the last paragraph where John lists all the different things that wounded dogs get wrapped in. I haven't found that to be as true with horse owners. Horse blood has an amazing ability to clot quickly. Usually by the time an owner finds something to wrap a leg in, the blood has stopped flowing. In my 50 years of equine practice, I never saw a horse bleed to death. Any one of the materials that John talks about could potentially infect a wound. I was always happier if clients just let wounds stay open until I got there to clean and suture them. Sometimes first aid can be worst aid.

# Dr Jefferson: Equine Traditions

During America's early days, from the first settlers to around 1900, horses were the power that transported us, tilled our fields, and pulled the wagons that brought us goods. Knowledge about horse care was handed down through families. Many of the traditions and remedies have survived. Some are solid. Some are silly.

The first that comes to mind is how everyone, worldwide, is taught to approach and mount horses from their left side. Coming at them from the right would have worked equally well, but the left side is what horses are used to. Because they are creatures of habit, even more than us, this is a tradition that makes sense. A horse approached from the right is apt to shy. Imagine having to approach your dog only from one side. Dogs are more like, whatever, let's just play!

There was a Standardbred racetrack in Lewiston, Maine, until the late 1980s. It was there that I was first exposed to some of the old horse superstitions. I remember Charlie's barn in which there was a whole garlic bulb nailed to the wall in each horse stall. I asked him about it. The old horseman replied that it kept shipping fever away. I asked how he knew that. "My father always did it, and it's always worked for me," he said. When I suggested vaccinating his horses for flu to keep his horses healthy, Charlie scoffed. End of discussion.

At that same track I learned another thing not taught in vet school. In the racing community there is a prejudice about horses with white feet. The saying I used to hear in Standardbred circles was:

One white foot try 'em.
Two white feet deny 'em.
Three white feet, feed 'em to the crows.

There are a number of variations on that ditty to be found online. It is interesting that in some breeds like the American Saddlebred and the Clydesdale, white legs and feet are desirable because they make those horses flashy. True confession: in my years of practice, it really did seem like a white foot on a horse was more subject to the bacterial condition of feet called gravel. Just sayin' ... I have no numbers to back that up.

Over 40 years ago I visited a classmate who was a Thoroughbred race track vet in New York. His daily calls included working the backside at Belmont Park. One day I accompanied him on his rounds at that famous track. I was surprised at some of the old traditions that are deeply set in the Thoroughbred industry. For example, when Standardbreds are to be groomed and harnessed, they are always taken out of their stalls. On Thoroughbred tracks all horse preparation is done in the stalls. The horses are secured by a light chain that runs from their halter to an eye bolt screwed into the back wall. Administering medications, grooming, and any fussing with them is never, ever done on the barn floor. When I asked a trainer why they didn't take them out and crosstie them in the barn alley way like trainers and grooms of other breeds, he was amazed.

"Why, that would break their spirit!" If I asked the same question today, I'll bet any horseman on that track would say the same thing. Old ideas die hard.

There are a variety of liniments available for horses' legs. They fill the tack trunks of every race stable in the country. Most of the liniments have secret formulas, but almost all contain some iodine. It makes the liniments dark and pungent. The idea behind liniments is to increase the circulation to the legs. I often saw owners rub liniment on a newly injured leg. I never understood why anyone would put something warming on an already hot leg. It's like throwing gasoline on a fire. The thing to do for any acute leg injury in horses and people is lots of ice or cold water for a few days to cool things down. Then the liniments can do their job.

I remember some of the old timers on the track putting a slab of raw steak on a swollen leg and securing it with a leg wrap for 24 hours. It always seemed like a waste of good meat to me. I was never convinced that it did much except attract flies.

Curious horses are apt to get porcupine quills right on the sensitive end of their noses. Owners often called me to ask if they should snip the quills to let the air out so they pull easier. That's an old wives tale which doesn't help. Quills are hard to pull out because the pointed ends of quills have hundreds of tiny barbs just like those on a fishhook. The quills are hollow, but snipping them doesn't make it easier to remove them. If there were just a few quills, I'd tell owners to use needle nose pliers to try and pull them. It hurts, and most horses will only put up with so much of that. A nose full of quills usually means a vet visit and some heavy sedation.

Four leaf clovers and horseshoes have been thought to be lucky for hundreds of years. It is a tradition to nail a shoe over entrances. They are commonly seen in horse barns over stall doors. There is some debate as to whether the opening of the shoe should be up or down. Some say up so the luck doesn't spill out. Others say down so good luck pours out. When a new client was trucking a horse to my place, I always gave our road name and then would say, "Turn right when you see the horseshoe on the telephone pole." I never considered myself superstitious, but I was aware that I nailed that shoe a certain way, and never for a minute considered doing it the other way. That would have been unlucky! You're welcome to visit anytime to see which way it's nailed on.

There has always been interesting lore surrounding horses. Some of the traditions go back centuries. It's one of the things that made being an equine practitioner such a rich and interesting experience.

* * * *

Afterthoughts by Dr Hunt:

Old superstitions never die. Maybe that is part of the human condition.

Hotels don't have a 13th floor, people walk around, rather than under, ladders, and horse owners keep horseshoes over the stall doors. The world is full of dangers, so maybe, as a survival tactic, we have these superstitions and old wives' tales to make us feel more safe. Dave did a wonderful job letting us in the secret world of horse owners. The time honored treatments that at times go against all logic are fascinating.

I must comment on porcupine quills. First of all, I owe a debt of gratitude to porcupines. Their quills help send all three of my kids to college. I pulled many a quill over the years in the wee hours of the evening as emergency calls. Dog owners also had the notion that it was helpful to cut the quills before pulling them. Quills are actually modified hair, and as Dave pointed out, are not under pressure. Cutting the quills actually made it harder for me to pull them because they sank deeper into the skin.

# Chapter 17
## Out to Pasture

# Dr Hunt: Next Phase

What do retired vets do with their lives? One thing for sure is that you won't see me out in the proverbial pasture, leisurely grazing on grass on a sunny afternoon (actually, that doesn't sound too bad on some days). I tell people that being retired is the "best job I've ever had." That doesn't mean I didn't love my career, but being retired has relieved me of the day-to-day duties of running a business and the emotional and physical demands of seeing patients and clients, sometimes seven days a week. Almost 30 years of being on professionally takes a lot of energy; it was very rewarding but eventually got taxing as I got older. Now my job is to pursue my other interests, and so far, it has been rewarding. Veterinary medicine is still in the mix, though; you can take the vet out of vet medicine, but you can't take vet medicine out of the vet.

I have written three books, this one being number four. I produce two radio shows at WERU, a local radio station in East Orland, Maine. One is a weekly five minute short feature on topics ranging from COVID to the history of the horseshoe. My other show is a monthly one hour interview of a guest of my choice on any topic animal-related. I've interviewed authors, veterinarians, wildlife biologists, and fishery biologists to name a few. My radio shows and writing force me to stay current in vet medicine and allow me to share vet care in my own way with the public and have fun doing it.

I taught veterinary technician students for three years at York County Community College in Wells, Maine. I loved interjecting my 30 years of experience into the subject matter to make lectures relevant. However, the pandemic changed teaching dramatically and possibly permanently by replacing live classes with online and virtual classes. The connection with the students is gone, and that was why I liked teaching. For now, I am retired from teaching.

Retirement has also freed me up to fulfill non-veterinary interests I've had all my life. Although I would love to get back into coaching track, I find officiating track meets to be equally satisfying. Being an official gets me back into the track milieu without committing to the daily responsibilities of coaching. I love interacting with the athletes. High school track athletes are typically smart, polite kids that show good sportsmanship and yet have that whacky teenage demeanor.

My wife and I love to get up and go. Sometimes we go hiking for a few days up in the White Mountains or we plan an adventure like driving across the U.S. or going on cruises all over the world from Portugal to Australia.

People ask me if I miss practicing vet medicine and the animals. I do miss the people and pets I got to know and the satisfaction of seeing an animal get better with my help. Despite the wonderful times, the pressures of managing cases, the headaches of running a business, and emotional energy needed to stay upbeat and sincerely empathetic took its toll. I didn't want to become that "old grumpy vet." Now when I meet a dog or cat all I have to do is pat them on the head, smile and compliment the owner. Secretly I'm giving them a visual physical exam, but I keep that to myself. I can't help it!

*  *  *  *

Afterthoughts by Dr Jefferson:

Seems that we are both enjoying retirement. We both felt that when we did quit, it was time. I outlasted John by years. Young whippersnapper! It was John's idea to do a book together. He also came up with the title and most of the chapter ideas. Even though it's been his brains behind this book, I'm holding out for an even split on the proceeds and the movie rights. Right up through actual publishing we have been in agreement on the book's content and how it should look.

# Dr Jefferson: A New Career or Two

I wasn't sure I was ever going to stop working. In my early 70s I was still having fun being a horse doctor. Retiring seemed to me like a faraway country. I hadn't given much thought to the idea. Finally, at 75, I began to consider it. I started cutting back, and it took three years before I finally said goodbye. My special interest the last 20 years had been chiropractic and acupuncture work, which I really enjoyed, I kept up with that but dropped the routine vaccinations and emergency work. No more midnight colics or suturing up cut horses. Sleep had become more important to me. I backed off on the days I worked from five to three, and finally to just two days a week. Covid made practice unwieldy, and I fully retired.

I had always heard that when you retire you should find new interests to keep your mind and body live. As I was pulling back from full time practice, I accepted a teaching job at York County Community College. I met Dr John Hunt there. John is a retired small animal vet who, like me, had written books. We shared a class, he taught the small animal medicine part, and I taught the large animal section. We both enjoyed the teaching and the students. Then Covid made most of the teaching online. That took the fun out of it, so both John and I retired for the second time. We have become good friends, and at John's suggestion, we decided to write this book together.

As I said in the first chapter, I have always been fascinated by animals and, no matter what the weather, would rather be out there than in here. I love working around my farm. There are a number of tote roads through my woods, and I enjoy spending time improving them with my tractor. A man and his tractor, it's a beautiful thing. Together we put in culverts, spread gravel, and take dirt from here and put it over there. I also spend a fair amount of time cutting firewood from trees on our farm.

Our family no longer has animals because we spend winters down south. We have a place in Florida near our daughter, Tally, and her husband, Ernie. I get my animal fix hanging out with their dog and cat. Back at home a neighbor, a short walk up the road, keeps pigs, goats, chickens, and three big dogs so I'm not lacking for animal company.

We share our garden space with two neighbors, and last year relocated it into the horse round pen so that we don't have to share so much with our local herd of seven deer.

Bonnie and I are active in our church, and I do some mentoring there for some men looking for business advice. In the past I have taken part in the prison ministry program, but Covid put the brakes on that for a while. I am enjoying being on the board of the Maine State Society for the Protection of Animals and feel like I have something to contribute to that excellent organization.

I'm often asked if I miss practice. I now think of myself as a writer and not as a vet. Most of my writing is about horses and their owners, but the enjoyment now is in the sharing of those experiences. I feel blessed by my 50 plus years as an equine vet and wouldn't trade my experiences for anything.

\* \* \* \*

Afterthoughts by Dr Hunt:

Dave describes his retirement as a gradual transition from vet medicine to writing. If you read between the lines, though, he really hasn't retired from the one thing that drove him into vet medicine: being outdoors. Even when we talk on the phone, it's almost always after he has been doing something outside. He tells me that when he writes, it doesn't take him long to drop his pen and run outside to play in his garden. His writing, which I love, is a way he can share his experiences in the outdoors, be it veterinary related or not.

Did you know Dave has picked up a new hobby? Kite flying! When in Florida, he enjoys going to the beach to try some new-fangled kite. Do you sense a theme? He is outside doing something!

We may be both out to pasture as practicing veterinarians, but I guarantee we are discovering new adventures out in the paddock.

# About the Authors

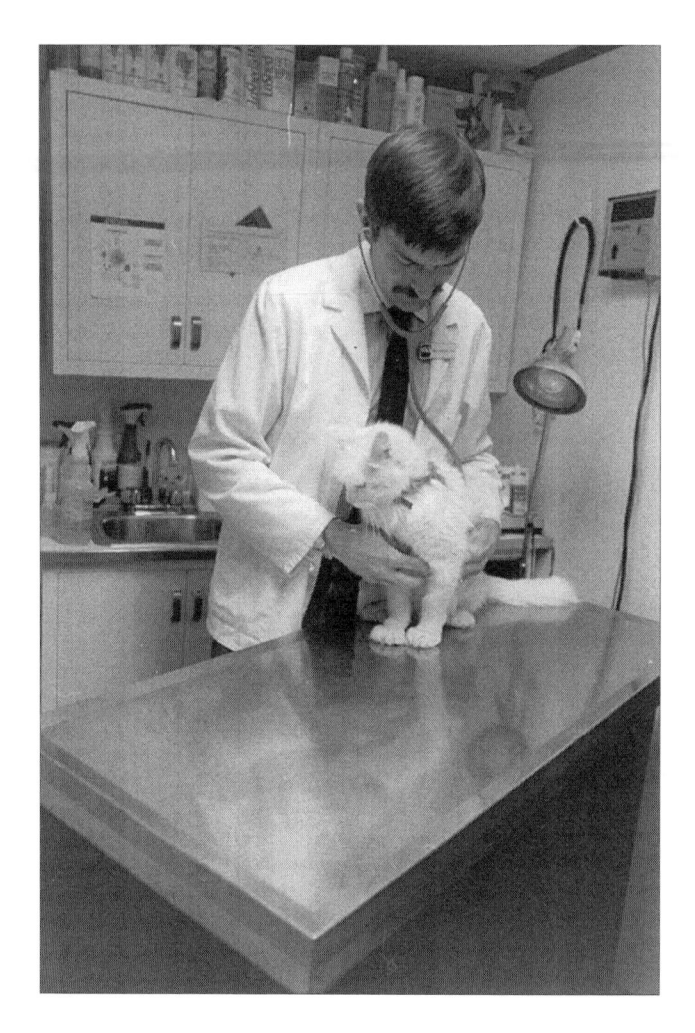

**Dr Hunt in 1994 at**

**Bucksport Veterinary Hospital**

# Dr John H. Hunt, Author

Dr Hunt practiced small animal medicine in Bucksport, Maine, for twenty-seven years. Prior to that he worked at three different vet hospitals in central Connecticut for five years. While in Bucksport Dr Hunt was a scoutmaster, coached middle school cross country and high school indoor and outdoor track, wrote for the local newspaper, gave talks at the elementary school, started a radio show, and acted in local musicals and plays. For a short time, he taught and was co-director of the Veterinary Technician program at the Bangor branch of the University of Maine, Augusta.

Dr Hunt sold his small animal practice in 2014 and moved to Eliot, Maine, in 2017 with his wife Michelle (a home care RN). Here he published two books, created a second radio show, officiates at high school track meets, and taught for three years at York County Community College Vet Tech program.

Besides writing, Dr Hunt enjoys reading, hiking, old movies, and traveling with wife, Michelle.

Hunt has three children, Will, Jane, and Molly, all grown. Will lives in Boston with his wife, Gergana, Jane lives in Portland, Maine, with husband, Noah, and their new daughter, Dovey, and Molly also lives in Portland with her significant other, Alex.

**Dr Jefferson with Draft Horses ~ 1972**

# Dr David A. Jefferson, Author

Until his retirement Dr Jefferson was the owner of Maine Equine Associates, an ambulatory equine practice. He is originally from Pelham, New York, miles from the nearest horse. His interest in horses began at Cornell University where he earned his veterinary degree.

Before college David served as an enlisted US Marine for three years. He attends the Vineyard Christian Fellowship of Mechanic Falls, Maine, and is part of their team that visits jail inmates. He has been a literacy volunteer, working with adults who have difficulty reading. Jefferson served as president of the Lewiston Auburn Rotary Club and the Maine Veterinary Medical Association. He is an active board member of the Maine State Society for the Protection of Animals. For three years he taught vet tech students their large animal courses at York County Community College in York, Maine.

David has been married to Bonnie for 56 years. They have two grown children. Their son Jim lives in mid-coast Maine and is an ecological cruise boat captain in Alaska during their tourist season. Their daughter Tally lives with her husband, Ernie, in St Petersburg, Florida, where they are in the real estate business together.

David enjoys writing and regularly submits essays about horses on his blog, ***www.HorsehealthwithDrJ.com*** He is also a weekly participant in a writer's group.

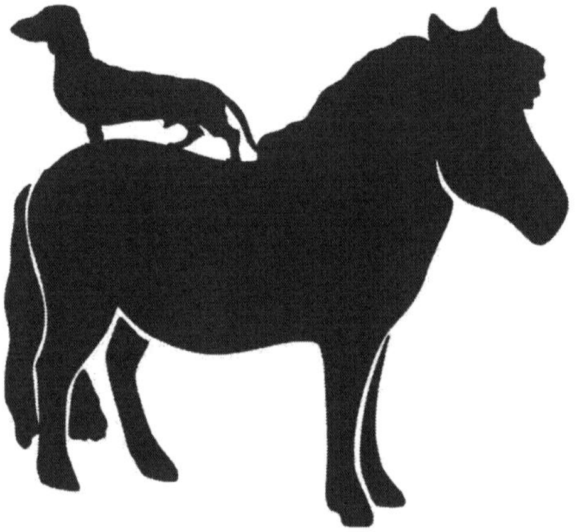

Made in the USA
Middletown, DE
24 October 2024